# CONTENTS

Acknowledgments . . . . . . . . . . . . . . . . . . . . . . . . . . . . . 5

Preface . . . . . . . . . . . . . . . . . . . . . . . . . . . . . . . . . . . 7

1 THINKING ABOUT ORDAINED MINISTRY . . . . . . . . . . 9
What's the Problem? . . . . . . . . . . . . . . . . . . . . . . . . . . . 9
Is There a Solution? . . . . . . . . . . . . . . . . . . . . . . . . . . 14
Some Basic Assumptions . . . . . . . . . . . . . . . . . . . . . . . 17
Who Is a Pastor? . . . . . . . . . . . . . . . . . . . . . . . . . . . . 19

2 SERVANTHOOD AND JESUS . . . . . . . . . . . . . . . . . . . . 22
Jesus' Servant Ministry . . . . . . . . . . . . . . . . . . . . . . . . 22
Servanthood as Theology . . . . . . . . . . . . . . . . . . . . . . . 27
Contemporary Critiques of Servanthood . . . . . . . . . . . . . 32
The Need for a New Paradigm . . . . . . . . . . . . . . . . . . . 37

3 SERVANT LEADERSHIP OF THE CHURCH . . . . . . . . . . 42
The Birth of the Servant Leader . . . . . . . . . . . . . . . . . . 42
Jesus as Servant Leader . . . . . . . . . . . . . . . . . . . . . . . . 44
Servant Leadership as Theology . . . . . . . . . . . . . . . . . . 48
Servant Leadership in the Church Today . . . . . . . . . . . . 51

4 A NEW THEOLOGY OF ORDAINED MINISTRY . . . . . . 61
Does God Exist? . . . . . . . . . . . . . . . . . . . . . . . . . . . . 61
The Trinity . . . . . . . . . . . . . . . . . . . . . . . . . . . . . . . . 62
Made in the Image of God . . . . . . . . . . . . . . . . . . . . . . 69
The Human Being Fully Alive . . . . . . . . . . . . . . . . . . . 73

No Longer Servants, but Friends . . . . . . . . . . . . . . . . . . . 75
Ordination, Baptism, and the Church . . . . . . . . . . . . . . . 77

5  A NEW PARADIGM FOR PASTORAL IDENTITY
   AND PRACTICE . . . . . . . . . . . . . . . . . . . . . . . . . . . . 82
   The Paradigm of Friendship . . . . . . . . . . . . . . . . . . . . . 82
   Pastoral Identity  . . . . . . . . . . . . . . . . . . . . . . . . . . . . 83
   Pastoral Practice  . . . . . . . . . . . . . . . . . . . . . . . . . . . . 86
   Friends in Ministry  . . . . . . . . . . . . . . . . . . . . . . . . . . 89
   Snapshot Comparisons . . . . . . . . . . . . . . . . . . . . . . . . 90
   Suggesting Some Ideas for an Ecclesiology  . . . . . . . . . . . . 97

APPENDIX A
"No Longer Servants, but Friends"
   A Sermon Based on John 15:12-17 . . . . . . . . . . . . . . . 101

APPENDIX B
Guidelines for a Commentary on Your Denomination's
   Ordination Service . . . . . . . . . . . . . . . . . . . . . . . . . . 105

Notes  . . . . . . . . . . . . . . . . . . . . . . . . . . . . . . . . . . . . 109

# ACKNOWLEDGMENTS

I finished writing the book during the summer of 1998. That summer my wife, the Reverend Dr. Marian Y. Adell, and I moved from Enid, Oklahoma, to Dayton, Ohio. I taught church history and historical theology at Phillips Theological Seminary, and Marian taught worship and preaching there. Now I am teaching church history at United Theological Seminary, and Marian is dividing her time between teaching at United and pastoring a small church.

It has been a difficult transitional year with the relocation of Phillips to Tulsa and the dislocation of some faculty and many more seminary students. I first want to thank Marian for her love and support during that year. I also want to thank her most recently for all the hard work she did in organizing the move and then unpacking the many, many boxes in our new home. Her willingness to deal with all the details of moving freed me to write.

I also want to thank the participants of the Hispanic Writers Workshop, the group that first helped me develop the main ideas and structure of this book during our times together from 1996–97. The workshop was sponsored by the Association for Hispanic Theological Education, located in Decatur, Georgia. I want to single out the association for its generosity and hospitality, especially Dr. Pablo Jiménez, who was the Executive Director at that time. The workshop's host and mentor was Dr. Justo L. González. Those of us fortunate enough to work with Dr. González recognize what an honor and privilege it is to be in his presence. I am deeply indebted to him for his kindness and wisdom.

# PREFACE

There is a gap in the literature about ordained ministry today. Most of the books on the market about ordained ministry are really about church leadership. A trip to any bookstore will clearly show this. Books about church leadership, management, and administration abound. They are very good at helping students learn what pastors do and at explaining to pastors how they can do their job better, but church leadership texts do not offer a theology of ordained ministry that aids students and pastors in understanding who they are as pastors. So the emphasis is on the tasks of ministry rather than on the person, with a head, a heart, and hands, who is the pastor.

An accessible theology of ordained ministry is needed to fill the empty space on the pastor's bookshelf. This book will help fill that void. It will pay specific attention to theologizing about both who a pastor is and what a pastor does, because pastoral identity and practice must be congruent in order to work together in creative ways that complement each other.

A word of caution is in order. This book is not a helpful how-to manual that will lead you step by step into becoming a better church leader, manager, or administrator. Instead, this book is an invitation to you to stop, take a few minutes, and reflect upon who you are as a pastor, not just what you do as a pastor or how you might do it better.

The question for reflection—Who is a pastor?—will echo throughout the pages of this new theology of ordained ministry. It became central for me while I was teaching church history and historical theology at Phillips Theological Seminary in Enid, Oklahoma.

Each year a new crop of students began their journey to ordination and full-time ministry with us. Who were these students going to be in this new world of ministry? Who were they to be as pastors? Were they to be like the pastor they grew up with? Like the minister who was now their field education supervisor or denominational representative? Were they to be like us, the faculty? Now in seminary and serving a church, who were they? No longer did they describe themselves as restaurant owners, farmers, nurses, police officers, housewives, personnel managers, schoolteachers, oil rig operators, church musicians, or lawyers. They described themselves as pastors, but they were not sure what they meant by that.

Together we explored the question, Who is a pastor? Both in class and out of class, we worked with one another in order to better articulate how they understood themselves in this new, uncharted world of pastoral ministry. We asked and tried to answer a number of questions:

How have we adopted the biblical image of servant as a norm for clergy?

What claims are we making today when we describe ordained ministers as "servant leaders"?

What expectations of our seminary students and pastors are implicit in these images?

Are we asking pastors to be and act like God, something they cannot successfully do, so that they end up burned out, quitting the ministry?

Is this the self-sacrifice of servanthood?

Or are we forming pastors to be not servants but friends, called to love and befriend the world, knowing what Jesus Christ knows and, on that basis, doing even greater things with him and not in place of him?

Some of the insights and some of the formulations that are in this book emerged out of those conversations. Therefore, this book is dedicated to the students at the Enid Campus of Phillips Theological Seminary and written especially for those who join them in what can be one of the most overwhelming, intimidating, and joyous experiences a person can ever have—seminary.

This book articulates a theology of ordained ministry and constructs a new paradigm for pastoral identity and practice. I hope that this book will aid seminary students and pastors in examining for themselves the nature of ordained ministry so that they can articulate their own theology of it and then live it out faithfully.

# CHAPTER 1

# Thinking About Ordained Ministry

This book is about theology and ordained ministry. It asserts that pastoral identity and practice need to be understood and articulated theologically. As Douglas John Hall has reminded us, the church needs to think about its faith in order to confess it (state what it believes) and then profess it (live what it believes).[1] It is very important that this thinking, articulating, and living be ongoing at the congregational level as well as in judicatories and seminaries, because the congregation is the primary *locus theologicus*, or place for doing theology, and the pastor is a resident theologian with that particular manifestation of the larger church.

Thinking about ordained ministry leads to confession, and there is no better place for confession, for stating what we believe, than in corporate worship. Standing in the presence of God and with the household of faith, the pastor, as a priest with that particular congregation, offers praise and thanksgiving to God. The pastor prays to God with the people of God, not on behalf of them. Pastor and people together offer their common life as a "holy and living sacrifice," united with Christ and dedicated to service. Out of this worship and its liturgy, the public service or work of the people of God, ministry and service emerge. Worship is the beginning of ministry because it gives ministry both its direction and its energy. Hence we see how the pastor is also a prophet with the congregation, calling the household of faith to a life of action that has emerged out of its praying and pondering together.

## What's the Problem?

It comes as no surprise that a pastor is a theologian, a priest, and a prophet with a particular congregation. But all these ministerial activities or pastoral practices require an underlying pastoral identity. So far we have only indicated what a pastor does; we need now to ask who a pastor is.

Currently there are two images for ordained ministry that answer this question about pastoral identity: servanthood and servant leadership. They are both very popular and influential in the church. Servanthood is taken for granted as an image for ordained ministry because Jesus is the model for ministry for most people. As servants, pastors are somehow to be like Jesus. They are supposed to be very giving of their time and energy and always ready to correctly and meaningfully respond to a church member's need or crisis.

Servant leadership is a very attractive image for ministry for many other people because it appears to blend what most churches look for in a pastor: a caring person who can also run a church. Here the emphasis is on growing the church. Pastors who are servant leaders are competent caregivers, but they devote most of their time and energy to achieving their vision for the church. Because these two images, servanthood and servant leadership, are taken for granted as the two paradigms that define ordained ministry, the theological implications and practical ramifications of each have gone virtually unexamined. This book will examine both paradigms, offering a critique of the assumption that they are the only acceptable understandings of ordained ministry, and proposing an alternative model.

## The Servanthood of Jesus

When I ask the question, What is a servant? students almost always refer to Jesus as the one who came to serve and not to be served. He is their model for ministry. Right away we are in the realm of *Christology,* the theological term that deals with the question, Who is Jesus? In other words, if one defines ministry in terms of the person and work of Jesus, then one's view of ministry, and one's understanding of who Jesus is, will be tied to each other.

The answer to the question of who Jesus is says something about the student's own sense of pastoral identity and view of pastoral ministry because each student brings to seminary an implicit theology about Jesus that both shapes their sense of call and undergirds their view of ministry. Those of us who teach in this context hope to make that theology explicit so that it can be articulated, and when articulated, explored, reshaped, and nuanced. But since very few students are ready to critique the concept of servanthood as applied to Jesus, it is important to ponder other questions first: Is Jesus a human being? Is Jesus the Incarnate Word of God? Is Jesus both human and divine? What did Jesus do? What was God doing through Jesus?

Chapter 2 of this book begins with a careful examination of servanthood and its association with Jesus' servant ministry. Here I pay particular attention to the characteristics of his earthly ministry and their applicability to ordained ministry today. From there I go on to address servanthood as theology, by asking the question, What are we saying theologically when we assert that Jesus *as servant* is the norm, the standard, for pastoral ministry? I discuss the implications of such a position for a theology of ordained ministry.

It is helpful to expand our frame of reference for understanding what Jesus' servant ministry means, and how it applies to the practice of pastoral ministry today. As we think about this concept of servanthood, it is important to recognize that it means different things to different people. We need the opportunity to explore how people experience and interpret servanthood differently. To help address this issue, chapter 2 will continue with some significant critiques of servanthood by feminist, womanist, and *mujerista* theologians, since each of these groups experiences the downside of servanthood.

One of the critics of servanthood is Susan Nelson Dunfee. A feminist, Dunfee argues in her book *Beyond Servanthood: Christianity and the Liberation of Women* that the model of ministry as servanthood cannot and does not empower women because servanthood presupposes a "self" that can give up power for the sake of another.[2] Since women do not have "selves" as men do in our culture, servanthood maintains the oppression of women. It does so by creating a dependent relationship between the one who serves and the one who is served. In place of servanthood, Dunfee argues for friendship as a model for relationships since it presumes freedom and equality rather than dependence and control.

Jacqueline Grant, in an article entitled "The Sin of Servanthood," continues Dunfee's point, this time from a womanist, or black woman's, perspective.[3] For black women, especially black domestics and maids, servanthood means servitude to the dominant white culture. This dominant culture uses language like "servanthood" to camouflage the racism that oppresses black people, especially these black women. Grant proposes "discipleship" as a new model for the liberation of black women. To support her argument, she documents the powerless and dependent lives of black domestics who, because they are real-life servants, have traditionally not been allowed to be disciples.

In another article, "Un Poquito de Justicia—A Little Bit of Justice," *mujerista* theologian Ada María Isasi-Díaz, reminds us of the daily struggle of Latinas against exploitation, marginalization, powerlessness, cultural imperialism, and systemic violence.[4] One of her chief concerns is the way the "no greater love" passage in John 15:13 is interpreted. Isasi-Díaz argues, from the experience and reflection of Latinas like herself, for a change in emphasis. The "no greater love" message of Jesus is transformative in the everyday struggle of Latinas, not because someone dies, but because someone helps another to live. Chapter 2 ends with a further analysis of servanthood and a rejection of the way that the servant model favors individualism, values a "task" orientation above others, fails to empower others, claims that adversity always forms character, and honors heroic struggle.

## Servant Leadership

Unlike the situation with servanthood, there is a dearth of material that offers a critique of servant leadership. On the contrary, servant leadership enjoys center stage as the predominant paradigm for ordained ministry today. It is universally (and wrongly) assumed that the idea originated in the Scriptures, and that in particular it refers to the ministry of Jesus. And since too few students are prepared to construct a church budget, work smoothly with a church finance committee, or run a successful stewardship campaign, its associations with the leadership / management / administrative side of pastoral ministry are welcome.

I became very aware of servant leadership as a seminary professor teaching Doctor of Ministry candidates. The course I was assigned to teach was "Parish Ministry as Servant Leadership of the Church." To my surprise, these men and women with ten to twenty years of ministerial experience and accompanying records of achievement could not provide at the start of the semester any clearer answers to the question, Who is a pastor? than their counterparts in the M.Div. program. They could, however, tell me about servant leadership. For them, servant leadership meant that their calendars were full of church events, meetings, and obligations. There was very little time for family or for themselves. The result of all this servant leadership, this "go, go, go and do, do, do" theology, was that their spiritual and prayer lives were virtually nonexistent and their sense of self-worth was low. I got the impression that underlying such professional reasons for entering the D.Min. program as updating pastoral skills and having the time to read, study, and discuss theological issues were the more personal needs for a nonanxious presence and a little support from their peers.

Like servanthood, servant leadership as a paradigm for ordained ministry needs to be critically reviewed. Chapter 3 will analyze Robert K. Greenleaf's original conception of a servant leader. I will offer a critique of the popular notion of a servant leader as one who puts the needs of others before one's own. We will see a real divergence between the popular version of the servant leader that the church has latched onto, and what I am calling the "indispensable leader." It will be illuminated by a careful reading of Greenleaf's portrait of one of the great servant leaders of all time, Jesus of Nazareth.

After this, I will examine the work of three contemporary pastoral theologians who have recently written about servant leadership as a starting place for reviewing and recasting what are really power issues within pastoral ministry. One will address the issue of pastors feeling like doormats when their congregation views them as servants. The other will explain his concern that pastors have a tendency to want to control and dominate the church. Another will focus on pastors doing what is required in ministry.

Not unlike the liberation theologians who revealed the harmful effects of adopting servanthood as a way of structuring relationships in the church, the issues that these additional three theologians raise will show how ambiguous servant leadership can be to those who embrace it. Servant leadership uses the modifier "servant" to deflect its true intentions regarding the exclusive use of power by the servant leader. Our discussion of servant leadership will reveal that the popular notions that many of us have of it as a paradigm for ordained ministry are inaccurate, and that an emphasis on doing is characteristic of both servanthood and servant leadership paradigms. The preference for "doing" over "being" has led to a univocal focus on Jesus' earthly ministry of servanthood as a paradigm for ordained ministry on the one hand, and to an equally focused corporate CEO servant leader paradigm on the other. Moreover, the servant image of Jesus, when it is transferred to ordinary human beings, conjures up real-life experiences of dependence and powerlessness for several of the groups that make up today's church in the United States. Unlike the servanthood image, the image of the servant leader is clearly an image of control and dominance when it is applied to ordinary people, for it pictures the servant leader taking authority and power over others.

## Is There a Solution?

This book offers a real alternative to the paradigms of servanthood and servant leadership. Chapter 4 opens with the question: Does God exist? This is an important question because ordained ministry is more than a job; it is a calling to be in partnership with God. The Letter to the Hebrews reminds us that we first need faith in God before we can approach and please God (Heb. 11:6). In other words, without faith our ministries will come to nothing.

We continue our discussion about God by investigating God as the Trinity, beginning with a discussion of trinitarian imagery in scripture and worship. Then we explore the understanding of the Trinity as "a community of equals united in mutual love."[5] This identification of God as loving Trinity allows us to get beyond the exclusive focus on Jesus' earthly ministry with the unloved and turn to his other community of the Father / Mother and the Spirit. This perspective is critical not only for our understanding of who God is but also for our comprehending who we are as human beings made in the image of God.

When we see that we share with God a common structure, "a community within," for understanding who we are and what we do, then we have the framework upon which we can build our new the-ology of ordained ministry. From this point we construct a theology of ordained ministry that is vitally relational and that focuses on the creative, connecting, and complementary power of the love of God for humanity that is ours as grace, God's own self-giving. We con-tinue with a discussion of this new theology that is based upon John 15:12-15, the passage that declares that we are no longer servants but friends. The chapter ends with some suggestions regarding the relationship between baptism and ordination.

Chapter 5 constructs a paradigm of friendship that is an alter-native to the servanthood and servant leadership paradigms for ordained ministry. The chapter offers clear examples of how this new paradigm of friendship actually works in day-to-day ministry through a series of "snapshot" comparisons among the three par-adigms. The chapter concludes by suggesting some ideas for an ecclesiology congruent with the new theology and paradigm. This new theology of ordained ministry is important because it offers another way of formulating and comprehending a theological foundation for one's pastoral identity and practice. It is significant that it is trinitarian because the Trinity offers us a new lens for examining pastoral self-understanding and ministry. Since one's self-understanding (being) as a pastor affects one's ministry (doing), and one's ministry (doing) affects one's self-understanding (being), it is vital that seminary students and pastors have a clear sense of who they are, not just what they are to do. Problems such as burnout occur when our theological self-understanding is inchoate, or when it is in conflict with the actual practice of our ministry.

Both the new theology of ordained ministry and its paradigm for pastoral identity and practice address head-on the neglected issue of pastoral identity. Together, they offer in clear theological language and imagery as well as in realistic and practical applications, a very helpful way of understanding how seminary students and pastors can be congruent in their pastoral identity and practice. When con-gruent with pastoral practice, a pastor's self-understanding will have a greater opportunity to work together with his or her ministry, thereby complementing it in creative ways. As we all know, when "pastor" becomes a part of your self-identification and the focus of your ministry, you can take off the clerical collar or the liturgical stole but you cannot remove the name "pastor." Being a pastor is part and parcel of who you are, not just what you do.

This is evident in how you as a pastor relate to people. Denominational theology and practice regarding ordination may appear in some cases to raise the pastor above the people. People will often treat you this way, as somehow "closer to God," once they know you are attending seminary or that you have a "the Reverend" in front of your name. You will be the first to be asked to "say grace" at meals, even by siblings who never saw you as particularly "religious" before. In other cases, people will notice your behavior toward others in a way you never experienced previously. You will have to treat people equally well, rather than single any one out as a favorite. You will also have to listen and pay attention to everyone who talks to you.

As a pastor, how you regard the sacraments is also an important indicator of denominational expectations and understandings because you will have to interpret the rites and rituals of the church to members and nonmembers alike. How you view the sacraments comes in part from how you understand your own ordination. Your own ordination sets the stage for how you see ritual in the church. So, if you as a pastor have a low view of ordination, then you probably will have a similar view of Baptism and the Lord's Supper. A low view of ordination sees the ritual as the church's recognition of when God initially called you to ministry. Such an understanding usually goes hand in hand with viewing Baptism and the Lord's Supper as mere remembrances about what God has done in the past that you observe either because Jesus commanded that they be done or because they are closely connected to his earthly ministry.

However, if you as a pastor have a high view of ordination, then you most likely will have a comparable view of the sacraments. A high view of ordination sees ritual as a time when the Holy Spirit bestows gifts and graces for ministry upon the ordained person. This understanding usually issues in a comparable understanding of Baptism and the Lord's Supper as events when the Spirit is currently at work in the world. In each case, theology matters. Ordination, Baptism, and the Lord's Supper can point either to God's activity in the past or to God's ongoing activity in the present. Whether your theology is well thought out or "off the cuff," it makes a difference which view you choose because that view affects your pastoral identity and your practice of ministry. Is ministry what you do or what God does with you?

The book concludes with two appendixes. The first one is a sermon, entitled (appropriately) "No Longer Servants, but Friends," that I preached first at an ordination service of one of my former students, and later at a revival / renewal service for another former student. The second appendix is an outline for writing a commentary on your denomination's ordination service. This is a very illuminating assignment, because as indicated in the discussion above, the service of ordination is one place a seminary student or pastor can look to find out just what a given denomination expects from its pastors (how it understands pastoral practice), as well as how it views the nature of ordained ministry (pastoral identity).

## Some Basic Assumptions

Before we go any further, there are some basic assumptions that shape both the scope and the tone of this book. The first assumption is that theology takes place in the context of the church and emerges out of the church as a reflection upon its faith. We begin, therefore, with a faith that we do not fully understand and cannot fully express. We affirm Augustine's position that we begin with faith in order to understand God. We also affirm Bernard of Clairvaux when he said that we believe in order to experience God. So, our faith seeks an understanding of God and it desires an intimate encounter with God. Then our faith can be expressed concretely in daily life.

The second assumption takes its cue from the sixteenth-century Protestant Reformers. Theology must be rooted in and accountable to Scripture, the Word of God to the church. It is in the Gospel according to John that we will find Jesus' new message about who we are. Jesus tells us that we are no longer servants, but friends (John 15:12-15).

The third assumption is that theology must be attentive to the Holy Spirit, who continues to speak to the church through its history, traditions, and voices of liberation. Therefore, theologizing requires not only Scripture but also tradition as foundational.

The fourth assumption takes seriously the marks of the church that emerge out of the Protestant Reformation. John Calvin stated it this way: "Wherever we see the Word of God purely preached and heard, and the sacraments administered according to Christ's institution, there, it is not to be doubted, a Church of God exists."[6] Calvin's statement, which was not unique to him as a Reformer, reminds us that the central focus of ordained ministry is the worship of God. Today we call this focus the ministry of word and sacrament. It is out of word and sacrament that ministry to the world begins and grows.

The fifth assumption is that church, the Body of Christ, is constituted not by the clergy but by the "priesthood of all believers." The whole church is "a chosen race, a royal priesthood, a holy nation, God's own people, in order that you may proclaim the mighty acts of him who called you out of darkness into his marvelous light" (1 Pet. 2:9). The Reformation understood the priesthood of all believers to mean that there was no mediator or priest between the believer and God other than Christ. All believers had access to Scripture and could read and interpret the Word of God without interference. Thus, each believer became his or her own priest, and ministry became a function of this priesthood.

The sixth basic assumption is that pastoral identity and practice are fundamentally relational and not simply functional. As such, any paradigm for ordained ministry must acknowledge and involve a theology of *who* the pastor *is* (the pastor's "being") and not just a theology about *what* the pastor *does* (the pastor's "doing"). However, it has been the functional, "doing" side of pastors that has captured the attention of readers and therefore the interest of most writers.

The seventh assumption is that it is the community, the church, the Body of Christ, that creates healthy individuals, and not the other way around. This relational bias states that you know yourself in relationship, not in isolation. So we need to constantly stress the centrality of the church instead of the individual pastor alone. The pastor is not "set apart" from the Body of Christ at ordination, but rather is "set within" a particular manifestation of that Body at ordination, most likely a congregation. Thus, the emphasis is not on separation but on deep relationality.

And finally, the theology presented in these pages is for rumination, mulling over, correcting, developing, and enhancing as you bring your own experience, questions, and insights to it. I have created "a work in progress" (as ministry itself is) rather than a fin- ished statement about the nature of ordained ministry (which may not be possible in this postmodern age). And I invite you, the reader, to join with me in ·"collaborative theology," to work with me in developing this theology, whoever you are and wherever you are in ministry.

Collaborative theology is necessary because there cannot be a definitive perspective about ministry for both men and women or a universal view that takes into account the various racial / ethnic groups and cultures that make up the church in the United States. If there is only one view for men and women, it does not take a rocket scientist to figure out which view will most likely still prevail. If there is a universal view, then it is really little more than the domi- nant culture's perspective dressed up to appeal to a larger audience. I am much more interested in shared insights than absolute truth, exploration of common concerns than final answers, and tending to the topic rather than completing it. I also know that what I have to say here will not speak to everyone or reflect everyone's experience. We all approach pastoral ministry a little differently from our social locations. We all have different mentors, serve churches in many places, hold membership in varied denominations, read Scripture from a wide range of hermeneutical assumptions, design worship from varying theological presuppositions, and experience God in many ways.

## Who Is a Pastor?

Since the Protestant Reformation of the sixteenth century, pas- toral identity and practice have been based upon the theological position known as the priesthood of all believers. The Reformers rejected the Catholic theological position that a "special character" or mark was bestowed upon the minister at ordination by the Holy Spirit. The sacramental identity of the minister as priest standing in the place of Christ, especially in the liturgical context of the eucharist, was replaced by the Reformers with a functional identity that declared the minister to be different from the congregation only in terms of office or function, not in terms of vocation or calling. However, questions regarding the distinction between the ministerial priesthood of the clergy, conferred at ordination, and the common priesthood of all believers, conferred at baptism, persist even today. New boundary lines were drawn between the two beginning in the seventeenth century with the development of the professional class. Until recently, professionalization separated the clergy from the laity because of education and privilege. Now what separates us and why are we separated?

In my experience, both clergy and laypeople immediately answer the question, Who is a pastor? by listing pastoral activities. Pastors preach, lead worship, make hospital calls, teach Bible studies, run meetings, serve on denominational committees. Pastors do a lot. Somewhere along the line we have been taught to think of ourselves as consituted by job descriptions rather than constituted by relationships. One of my seminary students once told me about a nearby pastor who, although he was a husband, father, son, and brother, refused to describe himself in any terms other than pastor. He was a pastor and only a pastor. According to him, he had a job to do; he did not have any relationships. This story is admittedly a little extreme, but it nonetheless serves to remind us that many of us have a tendency from time to time to see ourselves as a list of activities rather than as human beings related to other human beings. Why do I emphasize the relational aspects of ordained ministry over the functional? Relationships are vital for renewing our physical, mental, and spiritual energy. When we pastor, we not only exhaust our bodies and numb our brains, we deplete our souls. Sometimes we "run on fumes." Without relationships we have nowhere to go "to tank up" and go out again the next day.

An obvious, but nonetheless crucial relationship is with God. It should come as no surprise that there are pastors who drive themselves to the point where they run on empty. This tells me that a relationship with God is not primary for them, as it needs to be for all ordained ministers. Without a relationship with God as central, we tend to rely too much on ourselves to get things done, to make a difference, to improve the church. We seduce ourselves into thinking that we can do ministry on our own and that God is necessary only in a crisis. But God is an everyday God who calls us into relationship during the mundane moments of ministry as well as during crisis care for the community. Because we take seriously "the God factor"—that is, God's participation in our lives and ministry—we will begin our new theology of ordained ministry by discussing God.

Nevertheless, there is still that drive in ordained ministry to control the results of our work. Taking as foundational the promises of God in Christ Jesus helps us to see that as pastors we are seed planters like Apollos and Paul. Paul plants, Apollos waters, but God gives the growth (1 Cor. 3:5-9). This book is not against the necessary tasks of ministry or church programs. It is against reducing pastors to functions when we are constituted by relationships. You can feed the hungry, give drink to the thirsty, welcome the stranger, clothe the naked, care for the sick, and visit the imprisoned, and still give up trying to control the results of those ministries. Paul teaches us in his passage in 1 Corinthians that it is the community that does ministry, not just one member of it. Trying to control the results of planting or watering is egocentric. Pastors must see themselves as grounded in the larger church community so that they, like Paul, can see that God does not do away with their ministries but perfects them.

# CHAPTER 2

# Servanthood
# and Jesus

Historically, the biblical image of the servant is very influential in shaping the mission of the church and its pastoral ministry. When the church describes itself and its pastors as servants, the church looks not to just any servant for its model, but to Jesus. Jesus is the Servant Lord who, according to the Gospel of Mark, "came not to be served but to serve, and to give his life a ransom for many" (Mark 10:45). To his disciples he said, "Whoever wishes to be great among you must be your servant, and whoever wishes to be first among you must be your slave" (Matt. 20:26-27). It is Jesus' call, ministry, suffering, and death that shape the paradigm of servant ministry for the church. Any discussion of servanthood and pastoral ministry must begin with Jesus.

## Jesus' Servant Ministry

Jesus' earthly ministry reveals several characteristics of servanthood that inform the church's understanding of pastoral identity and practice. These characteristics are: call to ministry, service to the poor and the needy, self-emptying, obedience, and self-sacrifice. It is appropriate to ask: How are today's pastors to conform to this paradigm? How are they to emulate the model of Jesus' ministry, which culminates in suffering and violent death? In other words, which of these characteristics of Jesus' earthly ministry are valid for an understanding of pastoral identity and practice and which are not?

## The Call

First, the pastor is called by God and shaped by that call. H. Richard Niebuhr still provides the classic definition of the call to ministry. He describes it as having four parts:

(1) the call to be a Christian, which is variously described as the call to discipleship of Jesus Christ, to hearing and doing of the Word of God, to repentance and faith, et cetera; (2) the secret call, namely, that inner persuasion or experience whereby a person feels himself directly summoned or invited by God to take up the work of the ministry; (3) the providential call, which is that invitation and command to assume the work of the ministry which comes through the equipment of a person with the talents necessary for the exercise of the office and through the divine guidance of his life by all its circumstances; (4) the ecclesiastical call, that is, the summons and invitation extended to a man by some community or institution of the Church to engage in the work of the ministry.[1]

In actual experience, a person can resist the call offered by the God for some time and have a career and raise a family. One reason for so many "second career" seminary students today is this delayed response to an earlier call.

The "call to ministry" is an interesting phenomenon. When I ask seminary students what it means to them, they without exception tell a story about how they felt drawn to ministry. Many times students feel called when they experience a special closeness to God at a place like a church camp. Other students identify a pastor or mentor who suggested ministry to them years earlier. They did not pay much attention to the suggestion at the time, but over the years found that they could not forget the conversation. Still others want to help people, especially after a life-changing event, and sense that ministry might be the best way. When these persons finally accept the call to ministry, they must discern and nurture their "gifts and graces," their God-given abilities for ministry. This is where pastors and church people play a significant role by helping folk who want to accept their call test its validity.

The call to ministry is the crucial first step in a process of discernment. It cannot be validated by the person alone, but must be approved over time by the larger church. Seminary students do not always appreciate the mountains of paperwork and the tiring inter-views with ministry committees until they see for themselves how well the system, with all its flaws, really works in readying many for ministry while suggesting appropriate alternatives for others.

## Serving the Poor and Needy

Second, the model of Jesus' servanthood shows that the purpose of ordained ministry is to serve the poor and needy, not to seek reward. One of the most significant experiences students can have in seminary is an immersion trip, which takes them to another culture to learn about and be with the poor. Such an experience removes students from familiar surroundings and often exposes them to a language that they do not speak or understand as well as different foods, smells, dress, customs, and living quarters. This immersion into another culture can open up students to new ways of looking at life. Most often they are deeply moved by the hospitality of their hosts. They feel an immediate acceptance and warmth that is some-times overwhelming because it is completely unexpected. During these immersion trips students begin not just to see how "the other half" lives, but, on a personal level, to experience a common bond among human beings. On a socioeconomic level, students also expe-rience firsthand the results of greed and injustice because they live with their hosts, rather than return to comfortable rooms at night. Afterwards, most students develop a tremendous desire to confront injustice and to make it right.

Many times during its history the church has taken the side of the culture and aligned itself with the power in control, be it political, military, or economic. Jesus' clear and powerful message that he is the one who is hungry, the one who is thirsty, the stranger, the naked, the sick, and the imprisoned can never be overstated (Matt. 25:31-46). It is incumbent upon the church to always hold its sur-rounding culture accountable for how it treats "the least of these."

## Self-emptying

Third, the call from God and the practice of ministry involve giv-ing up or "emptying" oneself. If this is understood as letting go of caring about the results of one's own ministry, in favor of caring for

Jesus in others, then I am for it, because letting go is one way to describe a mature faith. But this is not how it is generally understood. Self-emptying may only lead us to try to fill up the empty spaces in our souls with things that are harmful.

The temptation inherent in this third characteristic is its opposite: self-importance, ambition, or a desire for recognition. Instead of fully self-emptying or letting go of their egos, pastors can turn around and boast of their humility. A friend of mine once gave a very expensive coat to a homeless person. Do you know how I know about this? My friend boasted about the good deed he had done instead of simply giving thanks to God for all the good things that he enjoyed. In boasting he showed how much his ego meant to him. He was asking me to see how wonderful he was rather than see how cold the homeless man was. The coat was not the issue; my friend was.

Ministry is not known as a position that pays six figures. So to compensate for the expenditure of energy, lack of sleep, constant worry, and feeling unappreciated that can accompany ministering to real people, pastors and seminary students alike can crave a simple "good job" or a pat on the back. For seminary students this need sometimes takes the shape of almost killing themselves to get all A's in seminary. For pastors it may be a concern over how prestigious the church assignment is. It can also appear in wanting to be the most popular seminary student with denominational officials. When supervisors and mentors give in to their own comparable temptations, students find their own harder to resist.

### Master and Slave

Fourth, the pastor must obey God as master. The master / servant (slave) relationship is an ancient one. It requires that servants (slaves) give total obedience to the commands of the master. If the master is the congregation, a judicatory official, or even the pastor's family, then this kind of obedience is not what is called for in ministry. In ministry we are held accountable by the congregation and the judicatory for our beliefs and our actions . We only owe our obedience to God.

Accountability to congregations, judicatory officials, and families is a difficult concept for some seminary students to grasp, as it is for many pastors. But accountability is a good thing. It helps keep us honest about who we are and what we are doing. Sometimes we take on roles and responsibilities that do not belong to us. At other times we avoid the roles and responsibilities that do belong to us. Accountability helps us tell the difference.

Whether in a hierarchical system or not, students often start out by bucking accountability. They do not want anyone telling them what to do. They think they know how things really should be done. And, especially with second-career adults, they are used to running their own lives quite well, thank you very much.

Then there are instances when students are confronted with questions of conscience about what they see going on in their communities, in their congregations, in their denominations, or among their colleagues. They wonder whether they should confide in anyone. They are unsure about speaking up and risking being labeled complainers, whiners, tattletales, or something worse. But with a system of accountability in place, students have a person to talk to who will hear them and act appropriately. Without such a system of accountability, those in power, or those who want power, have no checks or balances on their actions or desires. Without accountability there is dictatorship and oppression.

### Self-sacrifice

Fifth, Jesus' death on the cross is a reality that pastors must deal with in some way. Sometimes the efforts put forth by the ordained minister will need to be heroic or entail self-sacrifice. This is a modern version of *imitatio Christi,* the imitation of Christ through self-denial. Protestantism has often considered the historical expressions of self-denial, such as routine fasting and other bodily mortifications, as extreme. But when a pastor so identifies with Jesus that emulating his earthly ministry is the goal, then this ministry of self-denial is itself extreme. We must not deny that Jesus Christ is alive and doing a new thing. We are to keep his commandments, chiefly the law of love that is the Great Commandment.

The extreme of self-denial is martyrdom. The church has held since its earliest days that martyrdom is not something to be sought; God chose who was to die as a witness to the faith. In the case of seminary students, they are far from martyrdom, but they do practice an odd sort of self-denial. They deny their feelings and they deny their stress. This "self-denial" leaves them open to burnout.

Many people do not know what hit them when they enter seminary. Others lose perspective when they face the demands of student churches. The church takes over their lives and their families, and their sense of self suffers. This is a pattern that I see often and that needs to be broken. Most helpful would be ongoing support organized at the seminary level for each of the three, four, or five years it takes to complete seminary education. This support would offer a place where students could ask and get help for their new life in the pastorate without risk of being seen as less than "perfect."

## Servanthood as Theology

By adopting the biblical image of the servant as it is associated with Jesus in the New Testament, the church identifies the life, ministry, and death of Jesus as its paradigm for pastoral identity and practice. This makes Jesus as servant the norm for ordained ministry, and it generates an implicit theology of servanthood that undergirds that paradigm. What are the characteristics of this implicit theology? How are we to respond to them?

### Who Jesus Is

When we identify Jesus as servant as the norm for pastoral ministry, we make a number of theological assumptions that have unfortunate results. First, if Jesus as servant is the norm, then we are led to focus on Jesus' earthly ministry for an understanding of *who he is*, and we inaccurately interpret Jesus' personhood. We cannot separate what Jesus does from who Jesus is. While remembering his earthly community of the poor, the downtrodden, and the outcast, we forget his divine community of the Father / Mother and the Holy Spirit. We neglect Jesus' vital relationships with the One who creates and the One who sustains. Jesus did not accomplish his mission on earth alone. He did it with the help of the Father / Mother and the Spirit. Neglecting the Trinity leads ordained ministers to minimize the shaping and empowering roles of the Father / Mother and the Spirit in their lives and ministries.

Generally, pastoral identity and practice focus not just on following Jesus, but on trying to copy who he is as well as how he lived and ministered. When pastors attempt this, they blur the boundary between the Creator and the creature. God and humanity are not identical, nor can they be. Instead, God chooses to relate to humanity in a very personal way in Jesus Christ, and humanity, in turn, is free to accept or reject that relationship. So, when we as pastors identify with Jesus in this way, we also try to remake ourselves into a distorted image of Jesus when we are already made in the image of God. We cannot copy Jesus; we cannot be Jesus. Jesus is both fully human and fully divine. Asking pastors to emulate Jesus as the norm in effect reduces Jesus to human status and ignores the risen Christ. This is a major negative critique of the servant paradigm for ordained ministry. Pastors do not follow just a great man who inspires courage and a deep commitment. They follow the risen Christ, who cannot be copied by any person. Crossing this boundary leads to disappointing and sometimes disastrous results.

One such result is spiritualizing the gospel. Emphasizing the pastor's identification with the divine Jesus misrepresents God's "preferential option for the poor."[2] Rather than identifying with this Jesus, the Docetist[3] pastor should identify Jesus with those in need, the hungry, the thirsty, the stranger, the naked, and the imprisoned (Matt. 25:34-40). Otherwise, it is easy to construe the real physical, social, and economic needs of people as less important than their spiritual needs. This "pie in the sky" theology promises that our reward is in "heaven" and that God will take care of the needs of this earthly life there.

Another result is the opposite of spiritualizing the gospel. It is historicizing the Word. If the Arian pastor identifies with the human Jesus in this case, he or she misunderstands the Word.[4] Rather than identifying with Jesus, the pastor should identify Jesus with the Word, the Scriptures. Otherwise it is easy to limit how Jesus still lives by making his present, ongoing life merely a metaphor and to equate both his resurrection and the community's memory of him only with our life and ministry now. Thus, spiritualizing the gospel denies human need and elevates the spiritual above the physical, whereas historicizing the Word claims that Jesus lives only in our remembrances and actions instead of in that Word we encounter and experience as him.

## Curing Instead of Caring

Second, when we accept Jesus as servant as the norm for pastoral ministry, we end up rooting our theology in service rather than in love. This would be fine if we really meant service in the old meaning of the word, that is, worship. But we do not. Service and love are not synonymous, as we will see when we discuss some contemporary critiques of servanthood. With a theology of service we become more interested in "curing," in getting something done for people, rather than in "caring," being with people and getting to know them first.[5] In this latter way, they can be a part of what gets done.

Ironically, since the professionalization of the clergy in the eighteenth century along with medical doctors and lawyers, we have emphasized that the ordained minister is to be "set apart" as one who can "cure." What I mean by this is that pastors are really "masters." Like medical doctors and lawyers, pastors have the ability to "fix things," to "make things better," because as servants, they are actually in control. Servants are people who, ironically, master specific tasks. That is why good servants are so valuable. They are actually "in charge" of their particular tasks. This mastery, this power over their work, also gives servants a certain authority. So, with this mastery and control, we should really rename servants as "servant-masters." Servant-masters are then ennobled because they "give up" something. They "empty" themselves of their ability to relate, and replace relationships with jobs or the control and completion of tasks. One reason that servant leadership may be such a happy alternative for some is that all power, control, and authority are maintained and that nothing is "given up." On the contrary, power is taken as we will see in the next chapter.

In the case of the servant-master, the pastor is viewed not as a person, but as a "job description." Often we hear that pastors cannot be friends with their people, because if your pastor is your friend, then he or she cannot be your pastor. This means that he or she cannot have the authority over you that comes with the job, the mastery of specific tasks and the acquisition of special knowledge that enables that "extra special" closeness to God. This is actually a contemporary form of gnosticism. This ancient heresy argued that salvation required "special" knowledge and that there were levels of "perfection" for human beings. The highest level meant being free from one's physical body and the cares of this world.[6] This elevation of pastors creates some interesting dilemmas.

The denominational committees and boards that ordain and evaluate pastors now look for "effectiveness in ministry." Since this "effectiveness" is difficult to define, these groups measure what a pastor gets done and how many "cures" a pastor has effected, measured by a growing church, a bigger youth group, a successful stewardship or capital campaign, or paying their apportionments or per capita on time. Little is mentioned about worship except perhaps increased Sunday morning attendance or the minister's recognition as a good preacher. How the pastor "cares" for his or her people, how the flock is tended, cannot be measured as easily, but it appears in the words and actions of love that the people show their pastor and one another.

### The Cross

Third, when we affirm Jesus as servant as the norm, we are left interpreting the cross only as a means of past suffering and redemption instead of as a new way for us to engage the world right now. When we proclaim the risen Christ, the cross is transformed into the image of how we are to relate to one another. What was originally a mechanism for suffering and death is now a means of friendship.

Jesus has invited us to take up our cross and follow him. He has invited us to engage in two different but intertwined relationships that are necessary and sufficient for human life. The first relationship is with God, the second with humankind and the world. Imagine the cross. The vertical beam, representing our relationship with God, is primary. It is like the vine that is rooted in the soil of God's great love for us. The horizontal beam, designating our relationship with one another and the world, is possible only because it is attached at its center to the vertical beam. The horizontal beam cannot exist by itself, floating in space. As a branch, it cannot exist separately from the vine. This beam could rest on the ground unattached, but then it would not be a "cross" that could be "taken up." In other words, taking up our cross indicates our willingness to center ourselves in a relationship with God and engage in a relationship that attaches us to one another and to creation. Taking up our cross is our willingness to be one of the branches on the vine that is new life in Christ.

Viewed in this way, Jesus' imperative that we take up our crosses and follow him does not inevitably lead to sacrifice and suffering. The relationships symbolized by the cross are characterized by love and can therefore lead to joy as well as sacrifice, and to justice as well as suffering. Reminiscent of the vine and the branches, the cross is eucharistic at its center. It beckons us to receive, and give thanks for, the gift of relationship with God, for being "engrafted" onto the vine of life that enables us to love no longer as servants but as friends.

## Diminishing the Self

Fourth, when we focus on Jesus as servant as the norm, we become preoccupied with diminishing, if not eliminating, the self. In an often quoted passage from Philippians, the apostle Paul tells us that the pastor and the church are to have "the same mind" as Jesus. Paul illustrates this "same mind" by describing Jesus as the one who, not wanting to exploit his divinity, "emptied himself." In this emptying he took "the form of a slave" (servant). And, as a slave, Jesus, "humbled himself," obeyed God, and then "died on a cross" (Phil. 2:5-8).

When we identify with Jesus' self-emptying, we are actually misinterpreting the biblical passage. We are guilty of incorrect exegesis. Jesus emptied himself of his divinity so as not to take advantage of it. We human beings have no divinity that we can discard. On the contrary, we have enough difficulty as it is being fully human. One of my favorite second-century figures is Irenaeus, Bishop of Lyon. He once said that "the glory of God is the human being fully alive." Can a human being be fully alive and be empty of self? To get rid of one's self is to cease to exist. Jesus is calling us not to nonexistence but to abundant life. If we take this passage of scripture seriously, then perhaps we need to empty ourselves of our pretense to divinity that some feel comes with the call to ministry or ordination and acknowledge who Jesus really is, fully human and fully divine.

This call for self-emptying also does not speak to women, African Americans, or Hispanics. Each of these groups reads the Bible and hears the call to ministry differently from the way outlined above. Women read the Bible and experience the call to ministry as empowerment, rather than giving up power. African Americans read the Scriptures and experience the voice of God calling them to liberation from

31

oppression. Hispanics read the Bible "in Spanish" and experience God's call as providing a home, a family, and a country for exiles.[7]

For many, the paradigm of servanthood described above reveals the understanding of Jesus held by the dominant culture. The dominant culture views Jesus as one who is all powerful but gives up that power.[8] This Jesus, then, becomes the framework for ordained ministers. To be ordained ministers we are supposed to give up some power. This accounts for the emphasis on self-emptying. In theory, the self and power are collapsed into one, confusing the two. The self should not be diminished, the exercise of power should be restrained. But is the self really safe? And is power really lessened? These are questions to which we shall return.

### Master / Slave as Normative

And last, when we promote the use of servanthood as the paradigm for ordained ministry, we enshrine the master / slave [servant] dichotomy as normative. We establish opposition as foundational and ensure adversarial commitments, as for example, in the exclusive membership of many of our churches, not to mention how we often use our pledges for self-maintenance. Because the word "servant" can just as easily be read as "slave" in the New Testament, then we need to take another look at what a slave was and is.

The master has total control over the slave. The master owns the slave. In fact, a slave is no better than an animal because the slave has no rights, no dignity, no freedom. No matter how well the master treats the slave, the slave still has no identity except as property. Is this the best paradigm for ordained ministry?

The paradigm of servanthood as a way of structuring human relationships has rightly come under fire from women who are very well aware of oppositional structures and the very great harm they can do in the church as well as in the larger society. We now turn to three women theologians for their sharp critiques of servanthood.

## Contemporary Critiques of Servanthood

Some significant critiques of servanthood and its implications have emerged from feminist, womanist, and *mujerista* theologians. These theologians offer us contextual or liberation theologies that begin with their cultural-historical context as white, black, and Hispanic women, respectively.[9] They claim that the place for practicing theology is not with the church leadership or the academy, but rather with the everyday lives of women as told in their stories. These stories are both the content of, and the method for, theological reflection about oppression and God's will for the oppressed.

Characteristically, these contextual theologies are not theoretical works. Rather, they are the frameworks for real efforts aimed at changing society. This point is crucial. Liberation theologies are not about forgiving private sins; they are about changing systems. Contextual theologies seek both the empowerment of the individual and the community through the dismantling of the oppressive system. So, feminist, womanist, and *mujerista* theologies are intrinsically social and relational, seeking justice and not just parity, as they work for both socioeconomic and individual change.

In liberation theology generally, the reflection process begins by identifying both an oppressor and an oppressed group. Then it focuses on where the Christian message has been used to foster that oppression. The next step is to search for where the Christian message may foster new insights for liberation that have been buried or gone unrecognized.[10] In each step, contextual theologies stress that each marginalized person and group reread Scripture, history, and theology through their own eyes, through their own experience and struggle, not through the eyes of the dominant culture. We need to keep in mind these five characteristics of liberation theology as we proceed through the critiques of servanthood:

1. cultural-historical context,
2. reflection/action (praxis) over theorizing,
3. relatedness rather than isolation,
4. socioeconomic changes and not merely changes of "heart"
5. rereading Scripture, history, and theology through one's own experience and context.

### Beyond Servanthood

In her book, *Beyond Servanthood: Christianity and the Liberation of Women*, Susan Nelson Dunfee calls women to wholeness and freedom. Writing as a feminist in the 1980s, Dunfee states that the whole discussion about servanthood operates on the premise that a self, or what we might call a sense of personhood, already exists in all individuals. She contends, however, that this is not really the case for women. In fact, servanthood does more than simply promote the second-class status of women, it also creates a dependency between the woman and those she serves. Dependency happens because women, as "selfless," are without the power to respond to the needs of others in a way that takes into consideration not only the other person's needs but also their own.[11] So women are dependent, on the one hand, upon those they serve because without them, women would have no identity. And, on the other hand, women are also dependent upon those who serve them, because women are needy and cannot operate out of their own centers of identity, out of their own sense of self. In short, a woman's identity is selflessness and dependency. By being in servant relationships and without real options, women are being "themselves."

Dunfee wants women to have the power and the autonomy to be truly themselves. This means choosing to care for others in a way that diminishes neither the caregiver nor the one who receives care. It also means maintaining the power and autonomy of both the caregiver and the care receiver. For Dunfee, Jesus makes this new relationship possible. He offered a new paradigm when he called his disciples to be no longer servants, but friends (John 15:15). Jesus is also calling women to be friends. Dunfee argues that friendship with Jesus empowers women by situating them within communities and not keeping them isolated. Jesus also bestows upon all his friends the knowledge, authority, freedom, and responsibility that makes them autonomous persons.[12]

Friendship, then, is the new model for calling women to wholeness and freedom. Friendship entails making choices, not blind obedience. Jesus' command to love one another describes, according to Dunfee, what freedom means—that is, not obedience but the power to act out of one's own self.[13] And friendship, with its love and freedom, creates solidarity among people that, in turn, promotes and sustains personhood. As Dunfee sees it, friends "love their friends into freedom" and "as a community of friends . . . seek not to serve but to befriend the world."[14] Dunfee's insights and construction are foundational for the alternative theology and paradigm for ordained ministry that unfolds in subsequent chapters.

## The Sin of Servanthood

Jacquelyn Grant, a womanist theologian, develops a critique of servanthood in a persuasive article entitled "The Sin of Servanthood and the Deliverance of Discipleship."[15] Her argument begins with the empowerment of African American women. Servanthood language historically has masked the real servitude of these women. Grant asks us to reconsider servanthood language because, for African Americans, it enables systems of oppression and suffering to continue.

In an investigation of black-white social relationships after Emancipation, Grant focuses on the life of domestic servants as a case study in the maintenance of the status quo of oppression. She documents how white women ran the household, while black women did all the work. This arrangement kept in place the dominance of whites and the submission of blacks. Moreover, since domestic service was considered private service, it was not regulated by law. This legal maneuver allowed white women the right to still consider black women as property.[16] It is ironic that, while black women performed what has been described by another as the "exhausting, back breaking, unceasing nature of household labor,"[17] white women still labeled their domestic servants as "childlike," "lazy," "irresponsible," "larcenous," "worthless," "dirty," "dishonest," and "incompetent."[18]

Grant convincingly demonstrates that servanthood and service have not led to "empowerment and liberation, but in fact ha[ve] insured that they not happen."[19] How, then, she asks, "does one justify teaching a people that they are called to a life of service when they have been imprisoned by the most exploitive forms of service? Service and oppression of Blacks went hand in hand."[20]

The sin of servanthood, says Grant, is maintaining the status quo by conditioning blacks to be victims / slaves and whites to be victimizers / masters through the use of unexamined servanthood language.[21] Grant has clearly shown that servanthood language implies a domination / submission model of relationships and must be replaced. She suggests "discipleship" as "a more meaningful way of speaking about the life-work of Christians."[22]

Grant's discussion of how servanthood language remains unexamined is very helpful for understanding the ease with which Jesus as servant has become the norm for ordained ministry for many. Its language has also gone unquestioned. Grant's lesson to us is that we should not assume a meaning until we take a very good look at what we think is being said.

### A Little Bit of Justice

In an article entitled "Un Poquito de Justicia—a Little Bit of Justice: A Mujerista Account of Justice,"[23] *mujerista* theologian Ada María Isasi-Díaz addresses the "no greater love" message of Jesus recorded in the Gospel of John that has so often been promoted as the ultimate expression of servanthood. Without specifically referring to servanthood, she brings us into the Latina world of *lucha*, or struggle, that has all the marks of servanthood. After attending an *amistad*, or friendship, celebration among her Latina friends, Isasi-Díaz tells us what "no greater love" means to them:

> For them "no greater love" is *not* a matter of dying for someone else but a matter of not allowing someone else to die. For them "no greater love" is a matter of worrying about their neighborhood instead of worrying about ways of making it out of the neighborhood. For them "no greater love" has to do with *un poquito de justicia*—a little bit of justice—that they think society owes the Latino community so "at least our children can have a fighting chance to survive the drug war." For them "no greater love" is nothing but the justice-demand that is a constitutive element of the gospel message.[24]

In short, "no greater love" is not about death but about life with justice. For Latinas, justice is very specific according to Isasi-Díaz. Justice is the end of oppression in a Latina's daily struggle with exploitation, marginalization, powerlessness, cultural imperialism, and systemic violence. Justice does not mean a simple apology; it carries with it economic restitution, the means by which Latinas and the Latino community can live.

In general agreement with Dunfee and Grant about the status and treatment of women in the United States, Isasi-Díaz goes a step further in her article by calling for the oppressor and the oppressed to come together in solidarity to undo oppressive systems. This relationship is one of mutuality. Isasi-Díaz calls it friendship. Each side of the friendship empowers the other, and this empowerment creates the power to transform society.[25]

Isasi-Díaz makes a very important contribution to the constructive theology of ordained ministry by insisting that the gospel is about life and not about death. She is courageous in departing from the usual interpretations of familiar biblical stories using the theological lens that Jesus Christ gives life and not death.

This section can be summed up by saying that these three liberation theologians reflect common claims and characteristics in their writings. Each writes out of a concrete cultural, social, and historical context. For each of them the establishment of justice, not the discussion of theory, is vital. In addition, empowerment is not empowerment if it is at the expense of the community. Therefore, strengthening the community by creating social and economic opportunities, along with overturning the systems of evil, is the primary goal, not changing individual hearts.

Each woman reexamines her surroundings and her tradition in light of her own, and her community's, experience. Servanthood, in contrast, limits her context to the dominant culture of white male America and its corollary context of corporate America. In the experience and reflection of these theologians, servanthood does not strive for empowerment, but maintains the status quo of dependency and uses the language of the good news to oppress.

These women offer profound commentaries on the use and abuse of servanthood as a paradigm for relationships. It is clear that each points to the need for a new paradigm.

## The Need for a New Paradigm

Students come to seminary with a faith in God and a real desire to serve, to be servants, to give themselves to something bigger than they. The paradigm of servanthood that they bring with them actually undermines their efforts and their goal. Servanthood becomes synonymous with stress for themselves, their churches, and their families.

As a seminary professor, I watched M.Div. students each semester get excited and all wound up in their churches, often to the neglect of their families, their studies, and themselves. Some of the male students would bring pagers and cellular phones to class, unable to sever the umbilical cord to their congregations for a few hours. I had to write into each course syllabus that students were to turn off their pagers and phones during class.

Other men smoked more and more cigarettes during class breaks to try to deal with their stress. The seminary provided for some free counseling sessions at a local center, and some students took advantage of this offer. In one class, when a student confessed to shortness of breath and other symptoms of stress, I spent the first thirty minutes of the class period teaching everybody a deep-breathing technique for relaxation.

Still other male students grew waistlines larger than their blue jeans really permitted. At one point the student council at the seminary wisely stopped making doughnuts available before the first classes of the day, and switched to low-fat bagels.

The female students had their own concerns while finding the courage to enter into the still male-dominated world of ministry. Some of the women had to find their own voice and learn to stop apologizing before asking a question or offering a comment. In the beginning, some of their male counterparts in the classroom made this difficult by reinforcing female stereotypes. On several occasions I had to publicly encourage a female student by telling her that her questions and comments were indeed important. Other women, especially those who knew their own minds and were articulate, found that some of their fellow male students did not take them seriously at first. But as students got to know and care for one another, warm and lasting friendships were born.

The paradigm of servanthood misunderstands what it is to be an ordained minister because it misconstrues both Jesus' identity and his ministry. The paradigm seeks to impose upon us the model of a courageous, selfless Jesus who died trying to help others. But the real Jesus is so much more than that. He is the fully human and fully divine Incarnate Word of God. To ignore this foundational faith claim of the wider church about the identity of Jesus is to reduce God to the level of moral exemplar, weakening our foundation for ministry as worshipers and followers of Christ. We have forgotten that our real service is worship.

With its focus on the person instead of God, the paradigm of servanthood that is presented to seminary students and pastors wrongly values the individual instead of the community, doing over being, giving up power instead of empowerment, adversity rather than friendship as formative, and heroic struggle as more important than the daily struggle for survival. The effects of such a paradigm make us less than we are because we spend so much time and effort trying to be more than we can be.

## The Individual Above the Community

The controlling feature of servant ministry is that it is a Lone Ranger approach. The value and contribution of laypeople involved in ministry are not included in its mind-set and therefore are not important. We have all heard of senior pastors who put down youth and who denigrate the youth program and its leaders. With this kind of pastor, the totality of "real" ministry rests only upon their shoulders. As the one in charge, it is up to the pastor to determine what is valuable and important. So the pastor decides, and the community abides by the decision. This unmistakably skews the gospel message that tells us that the church is the Body of Christ on earth. As the Body of Christ, the church is empowered by the Spirit to encourage various ministries by different people in the church for the benefit of the community.

## Doing Over Being

When the pastor is totally responsible for ministry, then pastoral ministry logically becomes task-oriented. There is so much to do when you have to do it all yourself. Being with people becomes a waste of valuable time. After all, what does it accomplish? The pastor is now indispensable, and results are all that matter. Any theology of grace becomes irrelevant. Time management is the key. Pastors forget all the times that Jesus went out into the desert to pray, to get away from it all and to recharge.

## Giving Up Power Instead of Empowerment

When the minister's mantra is "all power is mine," it is traumatic for him or her to have to give up some power and share responsibility. But when exhaustion and reality set in, it is time to ask for help. Sometimes pastors get into a cycle of changing churches every three to five years rather than empowering others for ministry. So after three to five years, with all of their tried and true ideas running out, pastors recycle themselves and their ministry instead of enabling the ministry of the people of God.

### Adversity Rather Than Friendship as Formative

With the adoption of the paradigm of servanthood, pastors inevitably see the practice of ministry as adversarial. Battle lines are often drawn when one group in the church takes issue with the views of the pastor or something the pastor did. Admittedly, there are dysfunctional churches, but even in healthy churches pastors can take the slightest suggestion or criticism as a threat to their leadership, their power, and even to their self-esteem. Pastors are caught in this bind, because this is how the game is played according to this paradigm. They do all the giving, and the congregation does all the getting. This imbalance leads to conflict. When it will erupt is only a matter of time. *It's me against them* becomes the slogan, rather than *How can we be faithful followers of Christ?* Asking this question at the start of a ministry, and then following up on it, takes people skills, a willingness to listen, and a pastoral paradigm that views others as friends.

### Heroic Struggle as More Important Than Daily Struggle

With this adversarial system built right into the ministry, and with a crucified Jesus firmly planted in the pastor's mind, who can blame a pastor who emulates the earthly life and ministry of Jesus for seeing ministry as a heroic struggle? Who can blame a pastor for translating that heroic struggle into a more culturally approved struggle like competition? In contrast, the daily efforts of many people to feed a family, pay the bills, or fight depression are not very dramatic. This kind of struggle does not have the impact of our cultural myths about an individual's heroic struggle against a foe, be it on the battlefield or the gridiron.

### Qualities in a Pastor

As I thought about the construction of servanthood as a paradigm for ordained ministry, it became apparent to me that the qualities most people want in a pastor are not really those of a servant but those of a friend. In pastors we want someone who is attentive to us, participates in our lives, and accompanies us on our personal journeys. However, we do not see pastors as friends, because we have paradigms, like servanthood, for pastoral ministry that keep pastor and people separate from each other rather than bringing them together. The desire for a relationship of "care" rather than "cure" is evident, though, when the chief complaint about a pastor is that he or she does not "visit" or does not "listen." The word then goes out into the community that the pastor does not "care," that the pastor is "unapproachable."

I will argue in chapters 4 and 5 for a pastor and a people who can help each other live a life that is characterized by the quality of their relationships, by the faithfulness of their living out the gospel, not by the quantity of work that gets done. We have forgotten that pastors and people are companions; they are people who "break bread together." It is in the breaking of bread that friends recognize that the stranger in their midst is the risen Christ, not the crucified Jesus (Luke 24:13-35).

# CHAPTER 3

# Servant Leadership of the Church

Many in today's church have adopted the paradigm of servant leadership as the norm for pastoral ministry. The description of the pastoral ministry of the church as servant leadership is so prevalent that no one questions its use. Its scriptural origin is assumed and its meaning is taken for granted. So we begin this chapter by asking two important questions: Where does the term "servant leadership" come from, and what does it mean? After that discussion we will explore its use by the church by asking these questions: How have some contemporary church writers understood servant leadership, and why has the church adopted it so uncritically and with such enthusiasm?

## The Birth of the Servant Leader

The term "servant leadership" was coined by Robert K. Greenleaf in 1977 with the publication of his highly influential book, *Servant Leadership: A Journey into the Nature of Legitimate Power and Greatness*. During the 1970s, with Watergate, the Vietnam War, and civil rights unrest, Greenleaf perceived a "crisis of leadership" in the United States, especially in its institutions. From his position as the Director for Management Research at AT&T, Greenleaf sought to reach beyond the walls of corporate America to address the need for leadership development he saw in every segment of American society. His answer was servant leadership.

It may come as a surprise, but Greenleaf's inspiration for servant leadership did not come from Scripture. His inspiration came from a novel by Hermann Hesse called *Journey to the East*. The main character in this novel, Leo, was a servant to a group of pilgrims. When he had to leave the group, so much confusion and disorder ensued that the group gave up its plans for a pilgrimage. Years later, one of those former pilgrims discovered Leo serving as the abbot of an important monastery. From this simple story, the idea for the servant leader was born. In Hesse's character Leo, Greenleaf saw a deep connection between leadership and servanthood. Leo was a leader because he could organize a group of pilgrims for a common purpose, and a servant because he knew and met their needs. Taken together, these two elements made him a great leader. But, as we will see, servant leader can also mean "indispensable leader."

In a famous passage from *Servant Leadership*, Greenleaf highlights the two reasons Leo was so effective. They remain Greenleaf's distinguishing marks for the successful servant leader today:

> [When servant leaders serve others,] do those served grow as persons? Do they, *while being served*, become healthier, wiser, freer, more autonomous, more likely themselves to become servants? *And*, what is the effect on the least privileged in society; will they benefit or, at least, not be further deprived?[1]

We may ask at this point the same questions of the pilgrims assisted by the servant Leo. Remember that when Leo left the group of pilgrims, they could not function without him and quit the pilgrimage. Did they become "wiser, freer, more autonomous, more likely themselves to become servants"? If one of them had, we can guess that he would have taken over the leadership position and organized the pilgrimage; then the pilgrims would have been on their way. This is just one of many contradictions that we will encounter when we explore more closely Greenleaf's paradigm of servant leadership.

Greenleaf clearly promotes the idea that leadership must include servanthood because great leaders like Leo focus on the needs of others as part and parcel of their leadership. In a later book, *The Servant as Leader*, Greenleaf reiterates his insight into leadership, that leaders must be servants first: "[The servant leader] is sharply different from the person who is *leader* first. . . . The difference manifests itself in the care taken by the servant—first to make sure that other people's highest priority needs are being served."[2] On the surface, these two often quoted passages from Greenleaf's most

43

influential books appear inspired directly by scripture, therefore, they have demanded the attention of readers in the church. However, a closer examination of how Greenleaf interprets and uses scripture reveals something quite different when we analyze his portrayal of Jesus as servant leader.

## Jesus as Servant Leader

Although Greenleaf does not find his inspiration for servant leadership in scripture, he does find an excellent illustration of it there. It is important to recognize at the outset that Jesus is not the source of the concept of servant leadership. Rather, Jesus becomes a servant leader like other great men in history.[3] Therefore, church leaders who promote servant leadership need to remember that servant leadership is not, in its origin, a Christian concept. If it were, servant leadership would not define Jesus, but Jesus would define servant leadership![4] Taken from the Gospel of John (7:53–8:11), Greenleaf tells the story of Jesus and the adulterous woman as an example of what a servant leader does: he has a vision or goal, devises a plan that will realize that vision, and then puts that plan into action, thereby achieving the goal. Greenleaf does not tell this story because it is a memorable one about the mercy of God for a miserable sinner. He tells it because it contains all the elements of an effective servant leader. The selection of scripture by Greenleaf is very telling and is worthwhile quoting at length. We begin our analysis by noting that Greenleaf begins with a description of leaders, not of servants.

> Leaders must have more of an armor of confidence in facing the unknown—more than those who accept their leadership. This is partly anticipation and preparation, but it is also a very firm belief that in the stress of real life situations one can compose oneself in a way that permits the creative process to operate.
>
> This is told dramatically in one of the great stories of the human spirit—the story of Jesus when confronted with the woman taken in adultery. In this story Jesus is seen as a man, like all of us, with extraordinary prophetic insight of the kind we all have to some degree. He is a leader; he has a goal—to bring more compassion into the lives of people.
>
> In this scene the woman is cast down before him by the mob that is challenging Jesus' leadership. They cry, "The *law* says she shall be

stoned. What do *you* say?" Jesus must make a decision; he must give the *right* answer, *right* in the situation, and one that sustains his leadership toward his goal. The situation is deliberately stressed by his challengers. What does he do?

He sits there writing in the sand—a withdrawal device. In the pressure of the moment, having assessed the situation rationally, he assumes the attitude of withdrawal that will allow creative insight to function.

He could have taken another course; he could have regaled the mob with rational arguments about the superiority of compassion over torture. A good logical argument can be made for it. What would the result have been had he taken that course?

He did not choose to do that. He chose instead to withdraw and cut the stress—right in the event itself—in order to open his *awareness* to creative insight. And a great one came, one that has kept the story of the incident alive for two thousand years: "Let him that is without sin among you cast the first stone."[5]

A cursory analysis of this passage reveals the servant leader's method, what Greenleaf calls "the creative process." It also reveals several characteristics of servant leadership that we will see have made it so amenable for use by the church. In the passage quoted above, Jesus demonstrates the three-step creative process of a servant leader. First, Jesus has a vision, in this case a vision about bringing compassion to people. Second, he devises a plan that, in this story, requires that he speak to the crowd and intercede for the woman. Third, in this story he realizes his vision by calling upon both the crowd and the woman to admit their own sinfulness and sin no more.

A more in-depth analysis of the passage reveals the details of this three-step process. In this particular biblical story chosen by Greenleaf to illustrate servant leadership, the vision of compassion requires that Jesus, *the servant*, listen to all the participants, taking into account their particular concerns. The mob reminds Jesus that the law states that the adulterous woman must be stoned. Although the woman is silent, it is safe to say that she does not share the demands of the crowd. This is the data gathering stage of servant leadership.

The second stage is when Jesus, *the leader*, quietly sits down and writes in the sand. As a leader, Jesus has withdrawn himself, or stepped back from the situation, in order to assess it. He analyzes the accumulated data that are the concerns of the people involved, thinks through the problem, and is open and receptive to a solution that will present itself as a way of resolving the situation. Greenleaf calls this openness "awareness of creative insight." Finally, Jesus as *servant leader* comes to a conclusion about a course of action that leads all the participants in a new direction. The servant leader Jesus exhorts the mob: "Let him that is without sin among you cast the first stone."

With this statement, Jesus as servant leader brings together his listening to the concerns of the people, his analysis and creative insight, and his act that accomplishes his goal. The woman is safe, and the crowd disperses. This story demonstrates Greenleaf's belief that Jesus is a superb example of a servant leader because he does just what a servant leader does—he puts the needs of others before his own.

But there is much more going on in this story as Greenleaf tells it. He claims not only that the paradigm of servant leadership explains Jesus' actions, but also that this paradigm can be found in all "great" leaders. What, then, constitutes a great leader? What do we learn if we look past the motto of servant leadership—of putting the needs of others before one's own? In short, what kind of leader is being recommended?

In the first paragraph of the biblical story retold by Greenleaf above, he claims that servant leadership is an enterprise for confident individuals. In facing stressful situations where the outcome is unclear, the servant leader has "a very firm belief" that "one can compose oneself" in order to see and think clearly. Here Greenleaf is describing an isolated individual who has "faith" in himself.[6] Near the end of his book *Servant Leadership*, Greenleaf describes faith as being open to "awareness" or to "new creative acts, for the receiving of priceless gifts," especially love.[7] But he further characterizes the servant leader as one who has "faith in the validity of one's own inward experience; faith in the wisdom of the great events of one's history, . . . faith in doubt, in inquiry, and in the rebirth of wisdom; faith in the possibility of achieving a measure of sainthood on this earth." This leads to, and emerges from, a "continually evolving awareness" of oneself.[8] So one's leadership is self-contained and self-sustained. Thus, the first characteristic of servant leadership is not really concern for the needs of others, but concern for one's own abilities in stressful, thought-provoking situations. Servant leadership, then, stresses individualism.

In the second paragraph, Greenleaf describes the servant leader as one who is goal-oriented. In Jesus' case, the goal is compassion. But if we look more closely, we will see that the servant leader is much more than goal-oriented. The servant leader has "extraordinary prophetic insight" or profound vision. This is not something that we all share to the degree that Greenleaf is extolling in Jesus, even though we, like Jesus, are human. Greenleaf is describing a particular kind of human being. His servant leader has an uncanny ability to grasp the possibilities of life with a deeper vision of what can be and then is able to bring it about. With this caveat, we obviously cannot all be servant leaders.

The challenge to the leadership of the servant leader (given in the third paragraph) highlights the necessity for servant leaders not only to meet challenges to their leadership successfully, but also to maintain a focus on achieving their goal. The servant leader meets the challenge, according to Greenleaf, by giving not just an adequate answer or direction, but the *right* one that keeps everyone moving toward the servant leader's goal. The challenge is directed not toward a vision of compassion, but toward the servant leader's *own leadership*. This is significant because the challenge frames the confrontation as a competition for who is *right*, not for who is *compassionate*. The real issue is who will win, not justice accorded to the woman caught in adultery or culpability assigned to the people with stones in their hands. So maintaining one's own leadership by winning in face of competition is the third characteristic of servant leadership.

In the next paragraph we see that Jesus is sitting, writing in the sand. Greenleaf describes this as the withdrawal, or stepping back, that is necessary for both clarity of thought and creative insight to appear. What is Jesus to do? What is the right answer? But this picture of Jesus sitting and writing in the sand tells us much more than this. This sitting back to wait patiently for insight after rationally assessing the situation marks a sharp contrast between Jesus and the crowd. Here we find a cool, calm, and collected Jesus over against a hotheaded, raucous crowd that is clamoring for blood. This antithesis is not accidental, but a self-conscious description of a major difference between a servant leader and his followers. Sitting while a tornado of activity swirls around him shows just how calm and confident Jesus is. Writing in the sand shows that his mind continues to work on the problem. Here we see that the servant leader is in charge and in command of his reason while the followers are disorderly and confused. Cool, confident, patient rationality is the fourth characteristic of servant leaders.

Jesus is seeking the right course of action that will fulfill his vision of bringing compassion to people. In the final paragraph, it is Jesus' mind that is again emphasized. Jesus, though human, is regarded by Greenleaf as a Great Mind. Servant leaders, then, also must possess superb intellects that arrive at the right answer in stressful situations. Such an emphasis on the mind can lead servant leaders to see other people not as whole persons, but as lesser minds! Surprisingly, we see this in Jesus' attitude toward the crowd. They are followers who would not "get" his logical arguments that compassion is better than torture. The crowd, however, responds to the reasonableness of his creative insight. They understand on some level that they, too, are sinners like the woman caught in adultery. So here we see that the servant leader has a superior mind and makes correct choices about what to say and do, thus achieving his goal.

## Servant Leadership as Theology

What is the implied theology present in these claims and characteristics of Greenleaf's paradigm of servant leadership? An exploration of the theological implications of Greenleaf's servant leadership model will help us see why the dominant group in today's church has adopted it as a paradigm for ordained ministry.

First, the individualism of the servant leader shows that such a person really has faith in himself rather than in God, a message that runs counter to the good news. It also places what one does over what God has done for the world in Jesus Christ. But this should come as no surprise. The servant leader appeals to the embedded rugged individualism that is still so prevalent in our culture, and it reinforces the Great Man Theory of history, which holds that individuals set both the direction for others and the course of events.

Second, individualism fosters a great divide between the pastor and the people by creating systems of hierarchy. This results in an operative ecclesiology that has ministry reside chiefly in the pastor, rather than in the church as a whole, the Body of Christ. By taking the responsibility for ministry out of the hands of the laypeople, the pastor alone is responsible. And the one who is responsible sets both the agenda and the measure of success. As we will see later, this implicit ecclesiology is neither scriptural nor the practice of the early church.

The goal-orientation and achievement-driven characteristics of servant leaders build upon this foundation of individualism and pastoral ministerial responsibility. In the old distinction between works and grace, individualism emphasizes "works." These works are the task, meeting challenges, having the right answers, making the correct choices, and achieving the goal. In Greenleaf's telling of the story about the woman caught in adultery, Jesus is faced not only with achieving his goal but also with successfully meeting the challenge to his leadership. The woman is incidental. She is merely the occasion for the challenge.

Like this human Jesus, the servant leader relies solely on his own abilities for solutions. Note that there is no consultation with the group; there are no checks and balances to the servant leader's power. Jesus hears their concerns, but as a group their concerns are univocal and their solution legalistic: the woman is guilty so she deserves stoning. That is all there is to it!

Although the scripture lesson from the Gospel of John sets up this dichotomy to prove a point about the abundant grace of God and the fact that all sin and fall short of the glory of God, Greenleaf uses the story for an entirely different purpose. Central Christian values such as community and interdependence are ignored. The priority in the church becomes the specific tasks chosen by the servant leader, not the people working together, empowered by the Holy Spirit. The end becomes more important than the journey and the companions along the way. In other words, people are secondary. Getting the job done is the priority.

The ethos of servant leadership also fosters a competitive attitude rather than a cooperative one. This competition, as seen in Greenleaf's story about Jesus, is competition for control of a given situation or person. It is a competition between minds. Let us go back to Greenleaf's own example of what Jesus does: he saves an adulteress, not by picking up a weapon and beating his foes but by literally outsmarting them. For her part, the woman does not participate in her own liberation; a man must free her. Though the leader may be a servant, the woman is still a slave. And since she does not speak in Greenleaf's retelling of the story, perhaps we are to believe that she has no mind. We do know that she has a body, the physical means for committing her sin. It is true that dialogue and cooperation with others is messier, less efficient, and less predictable than simply taking charge of a situation. In the end, the focus of this task-oriented, achievement-driven characteristic is really on the power of the ordained minister, not on the people and not on the outcome.

The final theological implication for Greenleaf's servant leadership paradigm has to do with rationalism. This paradigm holds up the logical mind as the only way of knowing, through what Greenleaf calls "awareness of creative insight." Any mention of intuition, the body, or the emotions is omitted. Though subtle, this emphasis on rationality is reinforced by Greenleaf's choice of stories about Jesus. The woman has committed a sexual sin and has no voice in Greenleaf's commentary. Only examples of logical and rational ways of looking at the world—namely, the laws and commandments of the people and the reasoning of Jesus—are admissible ways of dealing with life, according to Greenleaf's telling of this story.

### Implications for a Theology of Ordained Ministry

The implications for a theology of ordained ministry lodged within the paradigm of servant leadership set up the ordinary ordained minister more for failure than for faithfulness. This is because of the attitudes and practices that are implicit in servant leadership.

In the church, the servant-leader paradigm promotes an ordained minister as one who does God's work in place of God, rather than as a seed planter in the fields of God or as a cocreator with God. This is because of the basic premise of servant leadership. It reduces the ministry of the church, the Body of Christ, empowered by the Spirit of Christ, to one person who appears to follow Jesus and the example of his earthly ministry. But, again, the emphasis in Greenleaf is not on Jesus' earthly ministry, but on a generic brand of "indispensable" servant leadership. Remember, Jesus is just one example of an effective servant leader. If Greenleaf was really interested in promoting a life that imitates Christ, then he would be arguing for the servanthood of Jesus as a paradigm, not servant leadership. Servant leadership is not the same as servanthood. As we saw in the previous chapter, servanthood as a paradigm roots itself in emulating Jesus and his earthly ministry. However, as servant leaders, we are urged to emulate Jesus up to a point. We are not encouraged to "empty" ourselves of our own self-interest and to "follow" God's will alone, which is a hallmark of Christian service. We need to remember that, in fact, servant leadership is not a biblical concept as it is widely assumed to be. The dominant culture of the church has, without scrutiny, adopted a clever appropriation of the biblical image of servant by one school of leadership, which uses the biblical image of the servant loosely to veil and make more amenable one style of corporate management. Does the servant leadership paradigm for ordained ministry legitimize an understanding of today's church as a corporation that needs leadership instead of the living Body of Christ spoken of in scripture and tradition? What kind of power is being promoted with each? In spite of the adjective servant, servant leadership draws the church toward business paradigms, not toward Christocentric ones.

By what authority, then, does a servant leader lead? A servant leader takes authority or wins authority by outsmarting his rivals. His authority comes from within himself, not from outside himself. The authority of the servant Jesus is different. His authority comes from God, and this authority is shared with others. It is very telling that servant leaders do not train apostles and disciples who will go on to lead others. As we saw in the beginning of this chapter, when the servant leader Leo leaves the group of pilgrims, they are lost.

## Servant Leadership in the Church Today

We have discussed the claims and characteristics of servant leadership as well as its theological implications. We now need to inquire about how they have been appropriated or translated by the church. Then we can continue our questioning about the paradigm of "servant leadership" in the church today and why it is so appealing. As a starting place for thinking again about issues regarding pastoral ministry and leadership, I have chosen to examine the work of three church professionals who have recently written about the paradigm of servant leadership. One is a seminary professor in theology, another is a retired Episcopal bishop, and the third is a Christian educator.

Each of the three have authored recent books on church leadership. The books that have taken Greenleaf's ideas about servant leadership and applied them to the everyday world of ordained ministry are *The Soul of Ministry, Servanthood,* and *Growing in Authority, Relinquishing Control.* Each translates servant leadership into the images and idiom of the church, giving us some clues as to why the church has adopted this paradigm so readily.

### Servant Leaders Are Not Doormats

Ray S. Anderson, in *The Soul of Ministry: Forming Leaders for God's People,* begins his chapter "The Ministry of Servant Leadership" by stressing that servant leadership is not about the pastor being the servant of the people, but about the pastor being the servant of God.[9] This statement is prompted by what Anderson finds to be a common concern in pastoral ministry, that pastors who see themselves as servants fear that the people will view them as a "doormat" and will "walk over them." This attitude only leads to pastors getting back at their congregations by abusing them in the long run.[10] But this is the wrong attitude to have about being a servant. A servant leader, states Anderson, is a servant of God who receives from God the vision of the mission of the people of God.[11] This is step one in being a servant leader, and it follows very closely Greenleaf's idea that the servant leader leads through "vision." This vision requires "stewardship" of the "energies and resources" of the people because the servant leader is chosen by God to achieve a specific revealed purpose in that congregation.[12]

In addition to leading through vision, the servant leader also leads through the power of an action plan, what Greenleaf calls "creative insight." This is step two. The action plan uses "discipline against disorder" and "direction for the disorganized" in the life of the people of God, so that the will of God will be accomplished.[13] To illustrate his point, Anderson reminds us of the servant leadership of Moses, who "with the power of discipline came the power to lead through directing the people back toward the Promised Land in fulfillment of the vision."[14] We need only remember the servant Leo, whom we encountered earlier in this chapter, and what happened when he was no longer available to lead his followers on their pilgrimage.

The structure of servant leadership in the church, as designed by Anderson, mirrors the general framework described by Greenleaf. Anderson begins with the wisdom of God (what God wills for the people of God) that is made known to the servant leader in a vision and then is articulated in a congregational mission statement. Anderson calls this "the common sense of leadership," that is, God reveals God's will in a clear and direct way to the servant leader.[15]

The work of God is the action plan of the people of God guided by the servant leader. This is "the creative strategy of leadership," according to Anderson. The will of God is the fulfillment or execution of the action plan so as to make real the original vision. Anderson calls this stage "the consummation of leadership."[16]

As director and coordinator of the "energies and resources of the people of God" throughout this three-stage process, the servant leader acts as a "'faithful steward' of God's vision."[17] To summarize Anderson's understanding of the use of power in the ministry of servant leadership, it is worth quoting one passage at length. Note that the power belongs to the servant leader.

> The servant leader will be able to articulate more clearly than anyone else the vision of the people of God as a contemporary interpretation of its mission.
>
> The servant leader will be more closely aligned with the promise that leads to the will of God than anyone else, and will factor that promise into the planning process.
>
> The servant leader will lead others who are responsible for implementing the planning process into full disclosure of the promise, vision, and goals that he or she holds to be essential to the planning process.
>
> The servant leader will exercise power by empowering others to see the vision, work the plan, and reap the benefits and blessings of doing God's will.
>
> The servant leader, more than anyone else, will be an advocate for those who stumble and fall through their own failure or who are wounded by others through the process.[18]

The parallels between this outline of servant leadership and the one offered by Greenleaf in his rendering of the biblical story about

Jesus, the crowd, and the adulterous woman are clear. Both Anderson and Greenleaf share a similar understanding of the power of the servant leader, recognizing that it is not just a style of leadership.

In the first paragraph, Anderson states that it is the servant leader who articulates more clearly than anyone else God's vision for the people of God. This is Greenleaf's supremely confident servant leader. And like Greenleaf, Anderson is equally unequivocal in his assertion. Paragraph two tells us that the servant leader will include God's intent in the action plan because he knows God's promise better than anyone else. Here is the goal-oriented servant leader of Robert K. Greenleaf. Only the servant leader, as we are told in paragraph three of the passage, can show the church the necessary promise of God, vision, and goals for their mission. This is the servant leader designed by Greenleaf who meets challenges by having the right information to put into action. Then the servant leader will empower others to understand, implement, and benefit from the servant leader's interpretation of what God wills for that church. The superior mind of the servant leader is at work in this paragraph as Greenleaf intended it. Last, the servant leader will care for those who fall short in the process of achieving God's will for the congregation. This brings the outline of servant leadership full circle by alluding to the motto of servant leadership that lends itself so readily to acceptance and use by the church—of putting the needs of others ahead of one's own.

The servant leader can do all these things, states Anderson, because he leads with spiritual gifts, not only with leadership skills. Anderson asserts "the gift of the Spirit as the motivating factor in the exercise of power and authority." He writes: "With the gift comes the character of Christ" and the qualities of "humility, non-exploitiveness, servanthood, and obedience to the mission and will of God as those that exemplify Christ."[19] It is Christ who is the servant of God in that he exercised his leadership "in the power of the Spirit, not for his own self-interest or glory."[20] Of course, it is here that Anderson parts company with Greenleaf. God is not a necessary element in Greenleaf's scheme of things. But even with Anderson's inclusion of God in his description of servant leadership, his outline of the basic components of servant leadership in his work is remarkable in its allegiance to Greenleaf's original statement. This demonstrates how easily an understanding and practice of pastoral ministry can be collapsed into Greenleaf's servant leadership paradigm and then left unchallenged. One comment by Anderson is very revealing. He writes this about Jesus: "Reading the account of his ministry from baptism to crucifixion, one would surely conclude that Jesus was an effective servant leader based on this job description!"[21] In this single sentence we have an encapsulation of Greenleaf's paradigm. Jesus does the job of a servant leader, putting the needs of others before his own.

### Servant Leaders Do Not Control

Bennett J. Sims approaches servant leadership from a different perspective than Anderson. In his book *Servanthood: Leadership for the Third Millennium*, Sims sees the central issue that confronts pastors as their need to control and dominate, rather than the fear of being walked over as a doormat.[22] Sims seeks to address this issue and remedy its results by training pastors to become servant leaders. The task of servant leaders, "to honor the personal dignity and worth of all who are led, and to evoke as much as possible their own innate creative power for leadership," becomes the task of pastors.[23]

Sims follows this line of thought because of the way he reads Greenleaf. According to Sims's interpretation, the servant leader "concentrates on building up the people, not on polishing the system or the leader's self-importance. When this is done . . . the system will essentially build itself."[24] This is in keeping with the motto of servant leadership, of taking care of others' needs before one's own.

With Greenleaf's inspiration, and a newfound understanding of Jesus as one "who taught and lived the concept of servant leadership nearly two thousand years before,"[25] Sims established the Institute for Servant Leadership in Hendersonville, North Carolina. This institute realizes Sims's goal of training pastors according to a servant leadership paradigm. Sims writes:

> For the church, we held up the vision of livelier worship and more inclusive decision-making. We hoped for leaders who would see their churches as centers of steady life-changing prayer, constant learning, and daring dispatch. We hoped for clergy who would see themselves as servants for developing and deploying Christian people with a keen sense of God's care for the world, along with the courage to challenge greed and injustice and to work for peace.[26]

While these goals are laudable and worthy of pursuit by any ordained minister, Sims goes way beyond them and makes a great leap in his book *Servanthood*. He jumps from promoting servant leadership as a training program for pastors to servant leadership as defining "the very character of God."[27] With Jesus as "the prototype of the servant leader," Sims argues that "servanthood is the biblical key to God's identity."[28] The Christian God, as demonstrated by Jesus, is a "Servant God," not an imperial deity on a throne.[29]

First, we can immediately detect a confusion between servanthood and servant leadership as they are equated in Sims's statements. This equation cannot successfully be made as we discussed in the previous chapter. Second, the change from understanding God as king to comprehending God as servant has enormous ramifications for how pastors view and use power, which really is *the* issue in leadership for Anderson and Sims as it is for Greenleaf generally. Using servant leadership as his paradigm, Sims continues to confuse servanthood and servant leadership as he strives to reshape pastoral leadership in terms of servanthood instead of control and dominance. For him "servanthood is the chief modifier of the power implicit in all leadership."[30] He writes that the "ability to empower is what makes great leadership a servanthood: it awakens the slumbering power in the souls of others."[31]

However, we have seen in our earlier discussion of Greenleaf's servant leadership that it emphasizes more than the keen power of insight and persuasion that an individual has over a group. It also registers the servant leader's concern for maintaining his leadership over the group in addition to achieving his goal. Granted that Greenleaf ostensibly wanted the power and dominance to be used for the good of the whole, his paradigm of servant leadership can promote neither parity in church relationships nor the equipping and empowering of the whole people of God to minister. Servant leadership actually contradicts what Sims is striving for and the church's teaching of "the priesthood of all believers." This teaching means that all believers, as priests, can approach God in prayer and the reading and interpretation of scripture without the mediation of any leader.

So Sims falls victim to the trap of confusing servant leadership with the servanthood of Jesus. He makes the two terms, and therefore the two concepts, synonymous when they clearly are not. Like

Anderson, Sims shows us how easily the church confuses the biblical idea of servanthood with Greenleaf's ideas about servant leadership.

## Servant Leaders Do What's Needed

Celia Hahn, a Christian educator, picks up the image of servant leadership in her book *Growing in Authority, Relinquishing Control: A New Approach to Faithful Leadership*. Like Anderson and Sims before her, Hahn also confuses servant leadership with servanthood. While focusing on the earthly ministry of Jesus, Hahn still resorts to its antithesis, servant leadership. About Greenleaf she writes: "Captured by the vision of Servant Leadership, Robert Greenleaf emphasizes 'doing to the least': all our actions are to be tested by the question, 'Will it benefit the least powerful?'"[32] So, Hahn suggests, servant leadership is "doing what's needed," not "centering in the ego." Or, as the title of her book suggests, "growing in authority" means growing as servants, and "relinquishing control" refers to letting go of our egos. There is no description farther from the reality of servant leadership.

Hahn then highlights "the servant metaphor" that provides "my example in Jesus." She writes: "But the servant metaphor offers me a life-giving alternative: finding my example in Jesus, finding Jesus in the one who needs service, experiencing the joy and freedom that can come from *being servants to one another through love*, and finding that *I have what it takes to do what's needed*."[33] This is a very telling passage. One does not read in either Anderson's or Sims's book that they have discovered that they "have what it takes to do what's needed." They assume it. In her own words, Hahn reminds us of Dunfee's critique of servanthood given in chapter 2. Hahn shows us that she still expresses love through service. Her point of view encourages women to care for others without taking into consideration their own needs, which is, on the surface, the position of servant leadership: putting the other's needs before one's own. However, as both servant leaders and servants, women continue to be captured by an identity that is dependent upon others in their care. This contradicts Greenleaf's independent, confident servant leader who sees Jesus not as a paradigm but only as an example.

As Christian people, we see the word *servant* and immediately associate it with Jesus. Then we think of the Christian calling to love God and serve the neighbor. So, on the surface, any popular use of the term *servant* conjures up in our minds this familiar and accessible paradigm, obscuring its real use. But servant leadership also speaks to another deep impulse within us in our complex world.

Servant leadership, as a paradigm for pastoral ministry, reframes the tensions between the dominant culture and the alternative voices within the church today. For the dominant culture, Jesus is the principal historical figure in the Christian story and a heroic one. As the obedient "Son of God," he denied himself, did the will of his Father, and then suffered torture and death. This heroic Jesus is crucial to a masculine brand of Christianity, because he is used to make male ministers singular in their abilities, setting them apart from female clergy. A heroic Jesus defines male pastoral identity by his obedience, self-denial, and self-sacrifice.

Not unlike the Catholic Church, which openly asserts maleness as one requirement for entry into the priesthood, Protestants still privilege maleness as a norm for ordained ministry. While the Catholic Church may assert the priest's sacramental identity with the risen Christ at the altar, the Protestant churches promote the pastor's own identification with Jesus by emphasizing his earthly ministry as the norm. So servant leadership, when adopted by the church, is Protestantism's version of emphasizing the maleness of Jesus by promoting a paradigm for ordained ministry that is aligned with a view of males that has deep roots in our culture. This view teaches males that individualistic, task-oriented, competitive, and rational attitudes and behaviors are the norm and are to be rewarded.

We can see the effects of this view when we look at male and female pastors. We know that the clergyman who calls himself a servant leader has a very different self-image from that of the clergywoman who assumes the same title. Men understand that a servant leader is a leader who serves. We also know that women experience a servant leader as a servant who tries to lead. The inescapable reality for women is that men still recognize women primarily as servants and not real leaders. How many times has a woman pastor been asked to be the secretary and take the minutes of the meeting she chairs?

Leadership, then, is problematic for women because they are still not taken seriously in leadership positions in our culture. By contrast, the male minister, who sees himself as a servant leader, imitates Jesus by "emptying" himself of his self-interest in order to serve other people. Often he receives acclaim for his decision. The female minister is already "empty." She has no self-interest to give up, because society views serving people as intrinsically "feminine." In a clerical double standard, the male minister's servant status is temporary, because he is still a man. The female minister's servant status is permanent, because she is still a woman.

Servant leadership as the norm for pastoral ministry needs to be discussed and examined before it is assumed as the starting point for a theology of ordained ministry. Making assumptions about its meaning and taking it for granted is one way that the church confuses servant leadership with the servanthood of Jesus as a paradigm for ordained ministry. Many male ordained ministers identify with the servant leader Jesus as one who is all powerful and then gives up his power. But having power and then giving it up is far different from not having any to begin with. This is where feminist, womanist, and *mujerista* critiques can help us especially in understanding just what servanthood and servant leadership of the church are telling us.

Not unlike the paradigm of servanthood, servant leadership as a paradigm for ordained ministry is also unacceptable because of what it claims and promotes. It expects ordained ministers to identify with the gender of Jesus and his gender-based acceptable behavior, which men can do and women cannot. This paradigm asks men, by identifying with Jesus in this way, to do ministry by themselves, stereotyping the people in the pews and discounting the power of the Word. In reflecting the gender and racial / ethnic biases of our culture, servant leadership perpetuates alienating social roles when, as a paradigm for ordained ministry, it should be offering a critique of those same prejudices and establishing inclusive patterns for the church.

Servant leadership wrongly situates the power of ministry in the person of the minister and the effectiveness of that ministry in the social location of the minister. It creates the illusion of "the indispensable leader." Greenleaf demonstrates this when he depicts the servant leader not only as the one who has *the* vision, imagination, and the initiative to show the way for others, but also as the only one who can take them there.

Servant leadership is more than a popular name for ordained

ministry, it is a mask that covers and hides the real nature of power and authority for Greenleaf. As we indicated earlier, his servant leader is really a corporate CEO in disguise! Greenleaf's emphasis is really on the leadership abilities of the person and not on the followers. But this is masked because the metaphor "servant," with all its popular associations with Jesus, who, for many, would never raise his voice or lift his hand, is cleverly attached to the real focus, the "leader." Today's church seeks out leaders, managers, and administrators because in many ministries being a "pastor"—a shepherd and a guide—is not enough. The ministry of word and sacrament can sometimes lose centrality when the work of the church becomes meetings, events, and committees, rather than an extension of the real service of the church, the public work of the people of God that is worship.

It is dangerous, though, to impose the standard of servant leadership on the church. Servant leadership does not begin to comprehend how really new Jesus Christ's message of liberation is. When Jesus Christ declares that his disciples are no longer servants—that is, no longer slaves—but friends, he is doing a new thing!

Therefore, as a paradigm, servant leadership sets forth a governing pattern or framework by which ministry is interpreted as leadership first, and then servanthood. In so doing, servant leadership offers a very troubling misreading of Jesus. We look to him as our model of what a servant leader is and how we are to be and to act like servant leaders. But, if we are faithful to the servant texts about Jesus in the New Testament, then we will have to acknowledge that the term *doulos* should be translated *slave* rather than *servant*. So, if we follow the model of Jesus, then servant leadership really means "slave leadership." The sound of slave leadership, however, is anathema to our ears, given both our own historical experience of slavery and the unimaginable concept that a slave could lead. Perhaps we are being pointed toward another direction for insight, a direction outside the dominant culture of the society and the church.

CHAPTER 4

# A New Theology of Ordained Ministry

Chapters 2 and 3 critiqued servanthood and servant leadership as inadequate paradigms for pastoral identity and practice. These chapters also discussed the implications of each paradigm's implicit theology of ordained ministry. This fourth chapter constructs a new theology of ordained ministry. Rather than begin with a character in a novel as does servant leadership, or with the earthly ministry of Jesus as does servanthood, we begin with a discussion about the nature of God as Trinity. We start here because the church claims that God is triune and that we are created in the image of God. That image resembles the loving relationships within the Trinity that reach out to the world. This triune image provides the foundation for (1) our self-understanding as human beings, (2) a new theology of ordained ministry, and (3) a new paradigm for pastoral identity and practice. In short, we begin with our relationship with God, the one who shapes us and calls us to ministry.

## Does God Exist?

Before we move on, we need to ask the question: Does God exist? This is not a frivolous question. Eugene Peterson tells us that for many people "God is not so much a person as a legend."[1] Therefore, believing in God is crucial to this new theology of ordained ministry. Without a faith in God and a consistent witness to what God has done for us in Christ Jesus, and continues to do through the Spirit, the temptation is to see ordained ministry as a job, as a list of things that we are expected to do and paid to do. Most of us do our job as ordained ministers well. However, to do the job well, to meet a congregation's expectations, or to score high in "effectiveness" in ministry, we do not have to believe or trust in God.

Does God exist? Is God included in ministry as a partner, or do pastors alone just do what "works"? Is the "God factor" real in ministry? The Letter to the Hebrews reminds us that "without faith it is impossible to please God, for whoever would approach him must believe that he exists and that he rewards those who seek him" (Heb. 11:6). So ordained ministry requires faith in God and living out that faith. As I tell my students, faith or Martin Luther's "unshakable confidence" in God, is where we get the energy to do ministry. It is crucial to maintain continually a vital and engaging relationship with God, nurturing it well before a crisis hits. And it will.

So ordained ministry is not a job but a vocation. Vocation means calling. When one is called, one responds. The response in ordained ministry is not to a job but to a way of life often called *discipleship*. Today pastors are not ordained *apostles* or *disciples*, they are ordained *professionals*. The original meaning of the word *professional* was "one who professes" or lives out what he or she believes, what he or she confesses. Today a professional is one who is trained to do a particular job but with a sense of higher calling about it. We make vows before the God who exists and the community of faith when we are ordained, and these vows are for a lifetime. Ordination is not repeatable nor is it a "temporary job assignment."[2]

In this chapter we begin our development of a new theology of ordained ministry with the church's teaching that the Trinity best describes who God is. The Trinity, then, forms the foundation of who we are as human beings. We are created in the image of the triune God. From this realization that we share a common image with God, a new theology of ordained ministry will emerge. The chapter concludes with some comments regarding the meaning of ordination and its relationship to baptism.

## The Trinity

The author of 1 John tells us: "Beloved, let us love one another, because love is from God; everyone who loves is born of God and knows God. Whoever does not love does not know God, for God is love" (4:7-8). God, then, is "free, self-communicating love."[3] This means that God chooses to love, to be in relationship instead of isolated. God's desire to participate in human life is revealed to us in a way that we can grasp. God makes God's free, self-communicating love known to us initially as the Father / Mother who creates all that is. Then God makes this love known to us as the Son, Jesus, whose resurrection from the dead reveals that God has redeemed humanity and creation. And God makes this love known to us as the Holy Spirit, who sustains the relationship between God and humankind with the Spirit's pouring out since Pentecost. We know about this love of God because of Jesus who is the Incarnate Word of God. Jesus tells us about his relationship with the Father and with the Spirit and thereby reveals the Trinity.

How are we to understand God as Trinity, as one and three at the same time? We must remember at this point that the church's understanding of God as Trinity is a confession of faith based upon the revelation of God in scripture and in the experience and subsequent reflection of the wider church. The Trinity is not a description of scientific fact, nor does it pretend to be.

The church affirms that God as Trinity is the one God of Israel who self expresses as Father / Mother, Son, and Holy Spirit. As Trinity, God reaches out to the world as the Creator of all that is, the Incarnate Word, and the Holy Spirit poured out upon the world. This reaching out to the world is not just a past event that is commemorated in worship. It is a present and future activity that is celebrated in worship.

Now some will no doubt immediately object to this construction of God as triune because the words "trinity" and "triune" do not appear in Scripture. Therefore, any understanding of God as Trinity, the argument goes, is suspect and to be rejected because the term, and therefore the concept, is not biblical. Others will dismiss belief in God as Trinity as a starting point because the teaching is obscure in its technical terminology and unnecessary in its declarations since we have been "saved by Jesus." However, the church still maintains the term "Trinity" as the name for its experience of the Father / Creator, Son / Redeemer, Spirit / Sustainer, even though the specific term is not found in the Bible and is often cast in bewildering theological formulae borrowed from earlier times. Examples of how the church experiences God in these three ways, expressed in trinitarian constructions, can be found in both the Gospels and the Pauline epistles.

### Trinitarian Imagery in the New Testament

In the Gospel according to Matthew, we find an excellent example of trinitarian imagery at Jesus' baptism. The text demonstrates the connections among the "Beloved" Jesus, the Spirit of God, and the Father as a voice from heaven.

> And when Jesus had been baptized, just as he came up from the water, suddenly the heavens were opened to him and he saw the Spirit of God descending like a dove and alighting on him. And a voice from heaven said, "This is my Son, the Beloved, with whom I am well pleased." (Matt. 3:16-17)

In John's Gospel, Jesus tells his disciples that the Father will give them another Advocate who will stay with them. Again, this passage shows the overlapping relationships among Jesus, the Father, and the Spirit. It also connects us to the Father and the Spirit when we love Jesus and keep his commandments.

> "If you love me, you will keep my commandments. And I will ask the Father, and he will give you another Advocate, to be with you forever. This is the Spirit of truth, whom the world cannot receive, because it neither sees him nor knows him. You know him, because he abides with you, and he will be in you." (John 14:15-17)

The next example contains partial or implicit trinitarian imagery. Found in the Gospel of John, Jesus as the Word is linked with God at the beginning of creation. As we remember from the book of Genesis in the Hebrew Bible, the Spirit also hovered over the waters at the beginning of creation. Again, the connections are made among Creator, Word, and Spirit.

> In the beginning was the Word, and the Word was with God, and the Word was God. He was in the beginning with God. All things came into being through him, and without him not one thing came into being. What has come into being in him was life, and the life was the light of all people. The light shines in the darkness, and the darkness did not overcome it. (John 1:1-5)

Familiar trinitarian language can also be found in three letters of Paul, namely, Romans, and 1 and 2 Corinthians. In 2 Corinthians, Paul writes about three ways of relating that characterize God's blessing of humankind, namely, grace, love, and communion. The blessing is for many a standard benediction at Sunday morning worship: "The grace of the Lord Jesus Christ, the love of God, and the communion of the Holy Spirit be with all of you" (2 Cor. 13:13).

In his first letter to the church at Corinth, Paul writes about the missions or activities of the Spirit, the Lord, and God. Spirit, Lord, and God are held together as one in being while differentiated in activity. This statement also serves for many as one foundation for the different orders or functions in the church. "Now there are varieties of gifts, but the same Spirit; and there are varieties of services, but the same Lord; and there are varieties of activities, but it is the same God who activates all of them in everyone" (1 Cor. 12:4-6). Last, Paul writes in Romans about the power of what the church has come to call the Trinity that is present in our lives as we struggle to live out the faith. Here we not only see the connections between God, Jesus, and the Holy Spirit, we also see how they work in, through, and with each other. Through Jesus we have God's peace, and through the Spirit we have God's love.

> Therefore, since we are justified by faith, we have peace with God through our Lord Jesus Christ, through whom we have obtained access to this grace in which we stand; and we boast in our hope of sharing the glory of God. And not only that, but we also boast in our sufferings, knowing that suffering produces endurance, and endurance produces character, and character produces hope, and hope does not disappoint us, because God's love has been poured into our hearts through the Holy Spirit that has been given to us. (Rom. 5:1-5)

Although the word *Trinity* is missing from the New Testament, clearly there is very important trinitarian imagery in its pages. The imagery strongly indicates that the church, from its earliest days, experienced God as Father / Mother, Son, and Holy Spirit. The church then reiterates and reinforces this understanding and experience in its worship.

## Trinitarian Imagery in Worship

Still other sources of trinitarian language and imagery can be found in many liturgies of baptism and eucharist. The prayers of thanksgiving that emerged from the liturgical renewal in the Protestant churches in the late 1960s and through the 1970s are characteristically trinitarian in structure and imagery. This pattern is not contrived or accidental, but rather follows the rubrics of the prayers of the early church.

The structure of the eucharistic or thanksgiving prayer in both the baptismal and communion liturgies is triadic. As we bless the water poured in baptism, and the bread and cup distributed in communion, we give thanks to God in three ways: first, in praising God's mighty acts in creation and history; second, in recalling our salvation in Jesus Christ; and third, in calling upon the Holy Spirit to be active and present.[4] In eucharistic prayers, the Trinity is recognized as the one God. The Gospel accounts, the witness of the Pauline epistles, and the liturgies of baptism and communion demonstrate and celebrate the biblical foundation of the church's teaching about God as Trinity. These biblical narratives and prayers of the church show that the three names we commonly use—Father, Son, and Holy Spirit—refer to the ways God expresses God's own Self in the experience and reflection of the church. Now comes the hard question: So what? The answer is that the trinitarian relationships in God tell us not only about how the church experiences God, but also about who God is internally, in God's very being. The payoff comes when we learn about who God is, because we also learn about who we are. Because we are created in the image of God, we are created in the image of the Trinity. So instead of viewing the Trinity as an obscure theological concept to avoid, we need to reclaim the Trinity for our understanding of God, ourselves, and the world. The Trinity, then, provides us with the basis of our theology of ordained ministry.

## A Community of Equals

Currently enjoying a resurgence in scholarly interest, the Trinity has been described by some as "a community of mutuality,"[5] "a community of equals united in mutual love,"[6] and "self-expending, other-affirming, community-building love."[7] The emphasis on community, mutuality, and love within the Trinity is intentional. The three concepts signal the salient features of God's triune identity and activity as understood and experienced by the church. Community refers to the Father / Mother, the Son, and the Spirit alive together in intimate, loving relationships, though experienced as three, still as one God. Mutuality indicates that everything is shared equally among the three as one. There is no "chain of command" or hierarchy. And although redemption is attributed to the experience of God that we know as Jesus Christ, the Father / Mother and the Spirit also worked with him. Love is the essence of God's triune identity and demonstrated by the activities of the three, both among themselves and reaching out to us. These activities are giving, affirming, and building.

Father / Mother, Son, and Spirit together make up a society of three equals who are united, that is, who live within one another and who move out with one another into the world through love. This complicated idea is known by the technical theological term, *perichoresis*. Father, Son, and Spirit remain as one God while simultaneously each expresses love to the world in, with, and through one another. Let's think of it this way for a moment. We have all been taught to think in terms of historical sequence. For example, we have been taught that each story has a beginning, a middle, and an end. In addition, each story follows this pattern without exception. Using the example of stories in scripture, we can read a story about the Father who created, a story about the Son who saved, and another story about the Holy Spirit who remained to challenge and to comfort. This is known as diachronic thinking. This kind of thinking cuts up the continuum of time into history. History is time marked and cut up into small chunks, like stories that we can read and interpret independently, or one after another.

But there is another way of thinking, called synchronic thinking. Synchronic thinking bundles things like stories together rather than separating them into chunks as history. Here time has no beginning, no middle, and no end. This means that a story does not unfold over time, event after event, in historical sequence. Instead, the whole story is enfolded all at once in the same moment of time, and the whole story is told and revealed all at once. There is no past and no future; there is only present, only now. God, then, as Father /

Mother creates at the same moment that the Son saves which is also the same moment that the Spirit is poured out. There are no gaps between their activities because they are not different gods. A diagram will help illustrate the difference in the two kinds of thinking.

Diachronic thinking          Past → Present → Future

Synchronic thinking          PastPresentFuture

One way to begin to understand perichoresis is to put diachronic thinking and synchronic thinking together. Diachronic thinking helps us see that the Father / Mother, the Son, and the Holy Spirit each have a mission or activity in history. Synchronic thinking helps us to see that the Father, the Son, and the Holy Spirit work as one because they are one. These three expressions are one, and the one self-expresses as three.

This idea of perichoresis is vitally important to our understanding of the Trinity, ourselves, and how we are to minister. It shows us that we can be united within ourselves while reaching out to another at the same time. We can be completely focused on the other person because we are completely "at home" in ourselves. A line from an old United Presbyterian Church (U.S.A.) wedding liturgy can be used to describe this "home" within ourselves that sends us out in friendship. This home is where we "build a house where no one is a stranger."

Perichoresis is how God loves. God is united within God's own self as Father / Mother, Son, and Spirit, and moves out as Creator, Redeemer, and Sustainer into the world, all at the same moment. This presence and this movement express God's own self, which is love, because love "seeks a third."[8] God loves as the Father who makes new things, as the Son who connects things, and as the Spirit who holds all things together. These three ways exist within God because within God's own self, God seeks a third. God is not God without the Father / Mother, the Son, or the Spirit. So friendship is rooted in the very nature of God. God is love that remains love while going out to share that love with others. God loves the world to show us how we are to live. We, too, are to "seek a third." We are to befriend the world.

Using a human analogy, this means that love between two persons cannot be contained but, on the contrary, must be shared to be friendship. Love between two persons compels them both to go out toward others, while at the same time remaining deeply connected to each other. This experience of reaching out to others distinguishes love that mirrors the divine from romantic love, which seeks to possess and control the beloved. Romantic love cannot be shared. This experience of sharing, of being friends, shows that loving the way God loves requires one to be relational, participatory, and communal. In short, this kind of love requires us to be friends.

### Friendship in God

How do we define friends? Using descriptions of the Trinity given above, and analogously applying them to us human beings, we can say that friends are "a community of equals united in mutual love"[9] who show "self-expending, other-affirming, community-building love."[10] As friends, the Father / Mother, Son, and Holy Spirit remain intimately and constantly connected to each other (their "oneness" in "being") while simultaneously each accomplishes their ongoing mission or activity in the world (their "threeness" in "doing"). The Trinity cannot do anything without its "being," "oneness," or internal connection, nor can it be anything without its "doing," "threeness" or external activities. We, too, have our being and doing inextricably linked within ourselves and with one another because we are created in the image of the Triune God. We are to be friends with ourselves, with each other, and with God. And yet, as we have seen, we tend to overemphasize our doing over our being in our self-understanding as human beings as well as in our professional life as ordained ministers. We neglect the image of God within us and prefer the self-reliant image we project. The Trinity, therefore, is a particularly fruitful image for who God is, who we really are, and how God is calling us to minister.

## Made in the Image of God

Now that we have explored the trinitarian nature and expression of God, we are ready to use the Trinity to construct a theology of ordained ministry that will be the basis for a new paradigm for pastoral identity and practice. We begin by thinking about ourselves as human beings. The theological implications of the paradigms of ser-

69

vanthood and servant leadership do not take into careful consideration the nature of humankind. Some in the church begin with the
servant ministry of Jesus as described in scripture for the construction of a distinct form of pastoral identity and practice that prizes
self-emptying. Others in the church begin with Greenleaf's servant
leader, who grew out of a character in a novel and grew into a corporate CEO. I begin by asking the question: In what image are we
human beings created? I start with this question because pastors
need to remember that they are human beings, first and foremost.
None of them is a "god." Pastors need to affirm their identity as
human beings created in the image of God, the *imago dei*. As we saw
earlier, the church proclaims in its classical teaching of the Trinity
that God is triune. God is Father / Mother, Son, and Holy Spirit.
Pastors, then, as human beings, are created in the image of the Triune God, not in the image of the self-emptied servant Jesus and not
in the image of the corporate CEO servant leader. The image of the
Trinity within us is the new starting point for a new theology of
ordained ministry and its new paradigm. The triune nature of God
strongly suggests that we begin seeing ourselves in triune and relational terms and not in the univocal terms of servanthood or servant
leader. Neither servanthood nor servant leadership allows for friendship, because friendship is fundamentally relational and only secon-
darily functional. But Jesus tells us that we are no longer servants or
servant leaders. We are friends.

Chapters 2 and 3 have shown us some of the problems encountered when pastors see themselves as servants or servant leaders and
not friends. When pastors view themselves as servants, they create
themselves in the image of Jesus, who came to serve. But Jesus is
more than a servant. He is the fully human and fully divine incarnation of the Word of God. We human beings are not created divine.
There remains an unbridgeable gulf between God and humanity that
only God can bridge, has bridged in Jesus Christ, and continues to
bridge with the Holy Spirit, Christ's Spirit. The creature cannot be
the Creator. Being created in the image of God does not mean that
we are God.

Since we are created in the image of the Trinity, we can apply the
Trinity's ways of relating on a human scale to ourselves. We are not
the Father / Creator, the Son / Redeemer, or the Holy Spirit / Sustainer. So, what shape does the image of the Trinity form in us? How

do we talk about ourselves as a trinity? We look at how we defined and discussed the Trinity and then apply the idea of "a community of equals united in mutual love" to ourselves.

## The Community Within

Mirroring the Trinity, the image of God that we have within us, means that we are created to love, to seek a third, to befriend God, ourselves, and our neighbors. When we relate like God, we love not as disembodied spirits, but as real human beings with minds and hearts and bodies. I prefer embodied language because it speaks to the whole person. All too often theology privileges the rational or the spiritual and denies the body imagery that is vital for theology to speak to the widest Christian audience.

The "community of equals united in mutual love," or a trinity, within us can be described as head, heart, and hands. We can talk about the head as the place of our creativity; the heart as the center of our congruence; and hands as the means of our complementarity. But before we explore in detail this idea that each of us is a community, we need to remember that we are not completed communities. Rather, we are striving to be fully alive. Irenaeus, Bishop of Lyon in the second century, once said, "The glory of God is the human being fully alive." This is what we are aiming at, being fully alive in order to give glory to God. But being fully alive is not something that we achieve, although we strive for it. To paraphrase the medieval genius and systematic theologian Thomas Aquinas, we might say that God completes our efforts by grace, by God's own self-giving in love. God does not remove our efforts, God works with us to bring them to fruition. With this caveat in mind, we return to our community within.

As human beings with a "head," we are creative. We do not create *ex nihilo*, out of nothing as God does, rather we are born *bricoleurs*. As *bricoleurs*, we create things out of what we find around us. We might make something out of a canvas and a palette, ancient theory and a computer, or a conversation and a sermon. As human beings with a "heart," we are congruent.[11] We work at understanding who we are so that it can correspond to, and be in harmony with, what we do. We want to be at home with ourselves and not see a stranger in the work we do or in the way we treat other people. As human beings with "hands," we are complementary. We like to work with other people to bring about new things. We like things to be completed and done well. We like things to work. As human beings created in the image of the Triune God, we want to be truly creative, truly congruent, and truly complementary, and we want to truly glorify God and live fully our human lives.

Another way of looking at this triune community within us is taken from an ancient way of being in the world, monasticism. A shorthand saying for this way of life might be *lex credendi, lex orandi, lex vivendi* or the law of belief, the law of prayer, the law of life. Belief, prayer, and living a faithful life are united in one person and balanced as expressions of love toward God, the neighbor, and the self. Belief or faith leads one to trust or to have confidence in the promises of God. This attitude affects how you treat those you deal with each day, and it also affects how you see yourself and how you determine your priorities. Prayer maintains the triune relationship you have among yourself, God, and your neighbor. You pray to God, and in so doing become clearer about the joys and burdens on your heart and in your mind. This clarity and depth of feeling then leads you to pray also for people with similar concerns. Faithful living directs you to make time for God each day, to take the time to offer a word of encouragement or accountability to your neighbor, and to forgive yourself and affirm your humanity.

Although each of these outlines really pertains to all Christians, the overlapping, interwoven categories of head, heart, and hands are very helpful for ordained ministers in particular. For them, head is the image of faith seeking understanding, so lifelong learning and study is vital. Heart stands for worship, for faith experiencing God through word and sacrament. Hands depict service, reaching out to embrace the world in love and justice.

In each translation, these three embodied images are the basis for becoming a friend of Christ, no longer a servant, but one who knows what Christ knows and who then can go on to do great things as Christ did. Through head, heart, and hands, the Christian person comes to know Christ in the Word, in prayer and sacrament, and in the one befriended. And in knowing Christ, we come to know the Trinity. Of particular concern for ordained ministers is that these three aspects of the ordained person must be kept in balance, because when the head is emphasized to the detriment of the others, an overly rational faith may rule. When the heart takes precedence, emotion and feeling may govern. When hands are the sole focus, burnout may be the result. A diagram summarizes the various ways our inner community can be described. The diagram is not exhaustive. The reader may wish to add to it.

| Creator | Head | Creativity | *Lex Credendi* | Faith | Study |
| Redeemer | Heart | Congruence | *Lex Orandi* | Prayer | Worship |
| Sustainer | Hands | Complementarity | *Lex Vivendi* | Life | Service |

## The Human Being Fully Alive

When Jesus was asked to sum up the law, what we are to believe and how we are to live, he answered with a call to relationship, what we customarily call the "Great Commandment." He said:

" 'You shall love the Lord your God will all your heart, and with all your soul, and with all your mind, and with all your strength.' [And] 'you shall love your neighbor as yourself.' There is no other commandment greater than these." (Mark 12:30-31)

This call to relationship is a call to love—to love God, love the neighbor, and love oneself. The Great Commandment tells us to love because God is love. Unlike God, we are not love; we are human beings who can love. So, as human beings who can and do love, we are constituted by relationships, good and bad, loving and hating, and everything in between. When we do love, love takes up and expresses our whole person as it does with God. With us, it is all our strength, all our mind, all our heart, and all our soul, not just a part of us.

The Trinity, with its loving relationships, and the Great Commandment of Jesus tell us that we have to love the many in order to love the one. We have to love God, our neighbors, and ourselves in order to truly love the One God, Who is Three. We cannot love God with our whole being if we do not love our neighbor and ourself. We cannot love our neighbor if we do not love ourself and God. We cannot love ourself if we do not love God and the neighbor. This is the larger story of what love is all about as set forth in the Great Commandment. To love only one or two and not three is not to love at all. It is to be in relationship only partially, that is, in a biased and incomplete way. And to love partially is to not know God fully and not to be the human being fully alive who God wants us to be.

As created in the image of God, we mirror the Trinity, albeit at a creaturely, finite level. As trinities ourselves, we are to love one another. We are to love our neighbors as ourselves. This little word *as* is very interesting. *As* means identification or equality. So if we love our neighbors as ourselves then we identify with another. Their joys are our joys; their sorrows are our sorrows; their needs are our needs; their dreams are our dreams. If we are to talk about loving our neighbors "with" ourselves, we only mean cooperating with them. We do not identify with them, and we have nothing in common with them. We may just work with them. Thus, unless we love our neighbors as ourselves, unless we identify with them, we may only cooperate with them or perhaps feel that we have some things in common. If we do not identity with them, there is no real imperative to love them. We can help them or ignore them. Either way, we maintain a level of distance that makes friendship difficult.

This brings us back to our understanding of God as Trinity and our understanding that we are created in the image of the Trinity. We must love the three in order to love the one. Here again is the whole story of God's love for the world. A univocal focus on the earthly ministry of Jesus, to the neglect of the Trinity, does not do God justice. How can we love the Son who redeems us and not love the Spirit who sustains us or the Father / Mother who creates us? How can we love the Spirit who sustains us and not love the Father / Mother who creates us or the Son who redeems us? And how can we love the Father / Mother God who creates us and not love the Son who redeems us or the Spirit who sustains us? Which one of the three, which two, can we do without in our theology? Can we live without the one who makes things new, the one who connects things again, or the one who holds all things together?

# No Longer Servants, but Friends

This new theology of ordained ministry is grounded in the faith claim that we are created in the image of the Triune God. As such, we share the same structure of our being and the same mission or doing as God, though obviously on a human scale. We, too, are a "community of equals united in mutual love." There is no sense here that we creatures have dispensed with the Creator. On the contrary, as human beings we exist to give glory to God and to be human beings fully alive. Fully alive human beings participate in loving relationships not in self-emptying. So much emphasis has been put on self-emptying and self-sacrifice by the individual rather than on the empowerment of all to full life. Dunfee, Grant, and Isasi-Díaz have shown in chapter 2 that enough empty selves already exist and want to be fully alive. In John 15:12-15, Jesus reminds us:

> "This is my commandment, that you love one another as I have loved you. No one has greater love than this, to lay down one's life for one's friends. You are my friends if you do what I command you. I do not call you servants any longer, because the servant does not know what the master is doing; but I have called you friends, because I have made known to you everything that I have heard from my Father."

In this passage of scripture, the emphasis for most people is on the statement, "No one has greater love than this, to lay down one's life for one's friends." This almost exclusive emphasis is one reason that the earthly ministry of Jesus has become such an influential paradigm for ordained ministry. So after this powerful sentence, the rest of the passage gets lost. But I think that the rest of the passage is as important as the first part. Jesus' crucifixion and death redeemed the world, reconciled us to God, and accomplished what we mere mortals could not. But redemption is not the end of the story. The story continues with the risen Christ and the church. Although "it is finished"—redemption has happened—we still have to be about the business of living it out because the world just doesn't get it! Jesus is calling us into relationship with the Trinity and with one another. He is calling us to construct a theology of ordained ministry that tells us that "we are no longer servants but friends." If we are no longer servants, what are we giving up? With servants or slaves, the relationship is obedience. The master has power over the slave, not "with" the slave, and certainly not "as" the slave. In ministry obedience may mean that we let the job or task define us. It has power over us. This is why I sometimes say to my students that they have given themselves to their calendars rather than giving their lives to God. They obey a calendar, not the living God. Because of this, I taught some students to schedule time with God, their families, and themselves on their calendars. This was the only way they would be sure to have the time to spend.

With friends, the relationship is love. Friendship exalts the power within each person to be free to love. Friends do not obey each other; friends love each other into being. And because love is an end in itself, friends are relational and not task-oriented with each other. So the new theology of ordained ministry is friendship rather than servanthood or servant leadership. When pastors view themselves as servant leaders, they create themselves in the image of the isolated leader who, relying upon his intellect alone, is driven to give the right answers, achieve goals, and maintain his own leadership and power. When pastors view themselves as servants, they limit their self-understanding and pastoral identity to a distorted view of Jesus. In so doing, they deny themselves access both to the Triune God and to the image of the Trinity that is within them.

Perhaps we can understand this astonishing friendship with God better if we explore one way God shares God's own self with us in the sacraments of Baptism and the Lord's Supper. Remember, God is "self-expending, other-affirming, community-building love." In baptism our relationship with God has changed radically due to God's activity. God has claimed us for God's own, and we cannot change the love God has for each of us any more than the prodigal son could change the love his father had for him. With this love we have been "sealed" or marked as God's own by the Holy Spirit forever. With this love we have also been "engrafted" or connected to the Body of Christ on earth, the church. The Trinity's relationship with us is not one of servanthood or servant leadership but of friendship. We are friends of God, and we are to be friends with each other. Baptism is the beginning of that friendship, and eucharist nurtures it in the context of the church.

The church is really not so much a "family," although most individual churches like to describe themselves that way. The church is really a community of friends that is "self-expending, other-affirming, and community-building." Friendship does not depend upon blood ties or marriage as families usually do. Friendship is open to the world as it crosses national, class, racial / ethnic, and even gender boundaries. Anyone can be a friend. Jesus tells us that we are no longer servants but friends, and the Trinity keeps empowering us for relationship by feeding us, keeping us alive in Christ, by the power of the Holy Spirit, through the eucharist.

## Ordination, Baptism, and the Church

The early church understood the practice of ministry as emerging from within the Body of Christ. Beginning with a discussion about the church as the Body of Christ in 1 Corinthians, the apostle Paul proclaims that there are spiritual gifts that are to be used for the common good. These gifts are well known: "utterance of wisdom," "utterance of knowledge," "faith," "healing," "working of miracles," "prophecy," "discernment of spirits," "various kinds of tongues," and the "interpretation of tongues" (1 Cor. 12:8-10). Paul then lists a variety of ministries that "God has appointed" (1 Cor. 12:28). They loosely correspond to the gifts of the Spirit: "apostles," "prophets," "teachers," "deeds of power," "gifts of healing," "forms of assistance," "forms of leadership," and "various kinds of tongues" (1 Cor. 12:28). Each of these gifts and ministries is "activated by one and the same Spirit, who allots to each one individually just as the Spirit chooses" (1 Cor. 12:11).

This early view of the church underscores the belief and the experience that the identity and practice of ministry emerges from and returns to the church, not individuals. Paul tells us, first, that it is the church as a whole, not just one or two people, that receives the gifts of the Spirit; second, that God determined and granted various ministries that are initiated and activated by the Spirit, not by any individual; and third, that both the gifts and ministries are to benefit the church, the whole people of God. Some people were ordained to specific ministries by prayer and the laying on of hands after being selected by an apostle. The laying on of hands was a sign of empowerment or setting apart by an authorized person.[12]

By the third century, this emphasis on a variety of gifts and ministries shifts to three ordained offices—bishop, elder, and deacon.

These offices are also bestowed upon individuals through prayer and the laying on of hands. Over time this three-tiered pattern of ordained ministry was expanded into several "orders," but for our purposes, we need only look at the priest, because this office corresponds to that of pastor, minister, presbyter, or elder.

In the medieval period, ordained ministry was primarily sacramental. At ordination, the Holy Spirit conferred upon the priest a sacramental identity and authority that put a Christlike mark or "character" within him. This character was especially evident in the liturgical context of the eucharist or holy communion. This was when the priest offered the sacrifice of the mass and consecrated the bread and the wine so that they became the body and blood of Christ as the words of institution were said.

In revolt against this teaching of the Catholic Church that seemed to locate Christ within the priest, the Protestant Reformation of the sixteenth century relocated Christ within the church as a whole, "the priesthood of all believers." The Reformers rejected the sacramental identity of the priest, and they replaced it with the functional identity of the minister. The minister now was different from the congregation only in terms of function, not in terms of any superior calling. The functions of the ordained minister were preaching, the administration of the sacraments, and the care of souls. Through the preaching, sacraments, and care of souls, all were called to justification by faith through grace, to love the neighbor, and to lead a holy life. The early, medieval, and reformation periods of our church history offer significant lessons for constructing a theology of ordained ministry.

We Protestants do the practical aspects of ministry very well. Perhaps this is another reason that the paradigms of servanthood and servant leadership are attractive to so many. We can organize a seminary curriculum for ministerial education; we can design a ritual for ordination; and we can efficiently place a minister in a church within our respective denominations. But when it comes to a theology of ordained ministry, we talk about a person's "call." Is it convincing? Is the person well adjusted? Can the person handle seminary? All the while we are thinking about the job description more than the inner person who is called to live a lifetime proclaiming the good news in word and deed, giving thanks to God for what God has done through Jesus Christ by the power of the Holy Spirit.

Since we view ministry as functional and not as a change of identity, as many do within the Catholic Church, we see no need to go beyond listing what a minister does. Even the prayers at ordination services do this. And yet we do not reordain a person when she or he changes denominations. Instead we focus on whether or not they have a good appreciation of their new denomination's "ethos." When someone leaves the ministry for some reason and then returns, we still do not reordain him or her. Our concern is whether or not the minister is psychologically "fit" to return to ministry or whether his or her "call" is still vital. So, it stands to reason that something in ordination "sticks." This "something" is missing in our thinking. How do we account for this something? We begin by retrieving some helpful clues from the church, the "priesthood of all believers."

The historic context for a Protestant ordained ministry is the priesthood of all believers because, by virtue of our baptism, we are all priests. We need no mediation between us and God. Baptism is a gift of God's grace that incorporates us into the Body of Christ, by the power of the Holy Spirit. This is significant because baptism recovers the image of God, the community of equals united in mutual love, within the person that was lost in the Fall. The person now relates to the Trinity in a new way by living in a new self-understanding, however inchoate, of that inward community that I am calling "head, heart, and hands" that goes out of one's self to seek a third and to befriend the world. The denominations that do not rebaptize do not reordain because they recognize ordination's connections to baptism, the necessary sacrament. What sticks, what does not need repeating, is baptism.

This new self-understanding and relationship made possible by baptism is transformative. It is prior to ordination; ordained ministry emerges from it. There is no special mark placed on the ordained person after the mark of the water of baptism, distinguishing the "ministerial priesthood" from the "common priesthood." Rather, after the perichoretic Trinity dwells within the person at baptism, this same person goes out from self in ordination in the specific ministry of word and sacrament. As baptism is the Trinity's renewal and rebirth of the community of mutuality within the person, ordination is one way that the Trinity can move out of the person who vows to publicly witness to God through the activities we call word and sacrament. Ordination is also the church's reminder to itself to befriend the world through worship and care, making available to all the means of grace and the friendship of the people of God under the guidance of a pastor.

For these purposes, the church authorizes some individuals for specific ministries, such as word and sacrament and friendship. The Holy Spirit continues to empower the person for that office by an ongoing uniting of the person to the image of the Trinity. So those who have been called by the Spirit to be *ordained* ministers must acknowledge that their ministry arises out of the priesthood of all believers, the church. Ordained ministry is not separate from the church but is accountable to it.

Baptism embodies a new self-understanding that undergirds this new theology of ordained ministry. The *self* is a community within a person that desires not to empty itself of its humanity but to fill its humanity with friendship with God, neighbors, and oneself. The community within wants to be fully alive in Christ by being truly congruent, fully alive in the Father / Mother by being truly creative, and fully alive in the Spirit by being truly complementary. As fully alive, the community of equals united in love within the human person glorifies God. No human self-emptying glorifies God unless the person empties himself or herself of servanthood or servant leadership and lives according to Jesus' statement that we are no longer servants but friends. Friendship is Jesus' paradigm for ordained ministry for us because it is trinitarian.

The claim of the priesthood of all believers and the theology of ordained ministry are resources for suggesting an ecclesiology, or doctrine of the church. As the baptized person and the clergy have communities within, so does the church. The church, as the Body of Christ in the world, dwells with the Trinity and goes out with the Trinity into the world. Moreover, the church is not a group of servants but a group of friends who, in seeking a third in love, befriend the world and call it to justice. The church does not call people to depend upon it, it calls people to relate to Christ and participate with Christ both in the communal, relational, participatory image of the Trinity within them and in the Trinity itself that loves them.

As the Body of Christ, the church has its own image of head, heart, and hands. Head, the domain of belief, is the area of the Word, preaching the good news, forming the person of faith together with the heart and hands. The heart, the domain of prayer, is the place of the sacraments and worship, connecting the person of faith together with the head and hands. And hands, the domain of service and hospitality, together with the head and heart, befriend the world. Here, like the baptized person and the ordained minister, the church loves God and the world with its whole self as it loves itself. Calvin had two marks of the church—preaching and sacraments. I am suggesting a third: not order or discipline, but friendship. For friendship goes to the core of *koinonia* or a community of equals united in mutual love within each of us and within the Trinity. Its original meaning encompasses fellowship and sharing. *Koinonia* is a partnership, a friendship that can empower friends to transform the world.

# CHAPTER 5

# A New Paradigm for Pastoral Identity and Practice

## The Paradigm of Friendship

The new theology of ordained ministry requires a paradigm shift from servanthood and servant leadership to friendship. Paradigm shifts are difficult to make because, as we have discussed, prominent paradigms often go unexamined. This examination, however, has revealed some significant problems in the current paradigms for ordained ministry, servanthood, and servant leadership.

The problem we have identified with the servanthood paradigm is its understanding of who Jesus is and how his ministry is to be used. The servanthood paradigm makes Jesus as servant the norm for pastoral ministry, with an emphasis on his self-emptying. The issue here is that pastors are urged to identify with who Jesus is, as well as to duplicate what he did. This raises serious Christological problems. Many of us domesticate Jesus by viewing him only as a historical figure. If we reduce Jesus to the status of a good man, then we reconstruct his life as the best moral example, whom we can then copy. However, if we affirm the church's teaching that Jesus is the Incarnation of God, then it becomes readily apparent that we can neither identify with God nor duplicate God's purpose and accomplishments individually.

There is a long tradition in the church of uniting with Christ. This tradition is grounded in the experience of the apostles in the New Testament and beautifully expressed by many saints of the church, such as Teresa of Avila and John of the Cross, in its later mystical literature. However, copying Jesus is not the same as uniting with Christ. Copying Jesus is about the person's own effort. Uniting with

Christ involves the power of the Holy Spirit. It takes form today in the recognition that the church, as the Body of Christ on earth, is, in fact, united with Christ by the power of the Holy Spirit and the love of God. The emphasis on human self-emptying is also a misreading of scripture, as discussed in chapter 2. Only Jesus, the Incarnate Word of God, can empty himself of God. By adopting the servant-hood paradigm, we are actually attempting the impossible, considering being fully human, as God calls us to be, is difficult enough.

The problem with servant leadership is that it wrongly requires that the pastor be indispensable because the vision, the authority, and the power for ministry are located within the pastor, not the church. We all know that the church existed before us and that it will exist in some form after us. None of us is indispensable. The problem here is that wisdom belongs to the clergy alone when the truth is that the Holy Spirit speaks to all kinds of people of faith, not just to the clergy. Moreover, ordained ministry emerges out of the church, the priesthood of all believers, and as such, is to be faithful and collegial, not fractious and controlling. The problems that arise when we adopt either the servanthood paradigm or the servant leader one urge us to propose an alternative paradigm.

This chapter will discuss friendship as a new paradigm for pastoral identity and practice based upon the theology of ordained ministry presented in the previous chapter. This chapter will also discuss how "no longer servants, but friends" actually works in a congregational setting, and it will give examples, as well as suggest some ideas, regarding an ecclesiology.

## Pastoral Identity

With this new theology of ordained ministry, the pastor can now see himself or herself as a friend rather than a servant or servant leader. This means that the pastor befriends God, other people, and himself or herself. There no longer is an emphasis on self-emptying or the diminishing of the person. Instead, the new emphasis is on being fully engaged with God, others, and one's self. As you remember, this is the new interpretation of the meaning of the cross for today. This interpretation does not do away with Jesus reconciling the world to God. On the contrary, it offers a real way of living in reconciliation and hope so that others may come to believe and have hope. The vertical beam is our relationship with God, the horizontal our reaching out to others.

| Servant | Servant Leader | Friendship |
|---|---|---|
| Copies Jesus' image | Is the CEO | Made in the image of the Trinity |
| Sees only tasks | Sees only self | Sees the whole person |
| Gives up self | Maintains one's power | Is fully alive |
| Fixes and cures | Achieves goals | Loves and cares |
| Masters specific tasks | Has the vision | Accompanies and participates |
| Authority | Control | Collegiality |
| Moral duty | Power | Vulnerability |
| Sacrifice | Effectiveness | Empowerment |
| Doing for others | Planning for self | Being with people |
| People as needy | People as functions | People as relationships |

The outline of the three paradigms above offers a summary of the chief differences among them. The friendship paradigm will help us begin to get out of dichotomous, "either / or" thinking that is implicit in the servant / master and servant leader / follower paradigms offer. By implementing a trinitarian view, this new paradigm frees us to begin "seeking the third" in friendship.

The friendship paradigm may require a real change in the theological thinking, as well as in the attitude and behavior, of some pastors. For other pastors, this paradigm may give them the language for what they are already doing. For still others, seeing pastoral identity and practice in terms of friendship may provide an alternative that was deeply desired. It is easy to see from the outline that the characteristics of the friendship paradigm distinguish it from the other two.

The outline of the friendship paradigm begins with the pastor recognizing that he or she is made in the image of God. This means that the pastor can be described as "head, heart, and hands." With the grace of our Lord Jesus Christ, the love of God, and the fellowship of the Holy Spirit, the pastor lives (1) the "head" aspect of a whole person by creating or putting things together through faith and study, (2) the "heart" aspect by holding things together through prayer and worship, and (3) the "hands" aspect by working together with others in life and service. This pastor understands himself or herself no longer as a servant or servant leader but as a friend.

As a friend, the pastor sees people as whole human beings who also are made in the image of the Triune God. As whole human beings, the pastor and the people are both called to be fully alive through relationships with God, one another, and themselves. There is no need to give up oneself when one is ordained, nor is it necessary to maintain one's power as clergy. Rather, pastor-to-people relationships are characterized by love and care. Gone is the "fix and cure," or the achievement of goals as the focus and force of ministry. In the context of a loving and caring relationship, the pastor accompanies (literally "breaks bread with") the people of God and participates in their journey through life. A vision for a program and the means to get it done do not supersede life together in faith, in worship, and in service. The pastor's ministry begins by being with folk as friends rather than doing for each other or making plans. It is in, with, and through these friendships that pastor and people love each other into full humanity. This is the basis for outreach into the community and the world. Jesus Christ died for our sins and reconciled us to the Father / Mother by the power of the Holy Spirit. That is finished. Now we have the opportunity to be cocreators with God by recreating friendship as the foundation for how we human beings relate instead of maintaining the dichotomies. Now we have the

85

opportunity to be cohealers with Christ by healing the brokenness of people that comes with being unloved. Now we have the opportunity to be coworkers with the Spirit by working to liberate people and social structures from hate and injustice.

The pastor who adopts the friendship paradigm is not only collegial, this pastor also does not need authority or control to be a pastor. To be fully alive is to be vulnerable and not to hide or deny one's own feelings and emotions or those of others. This pastor relies not on personal power or charisma but on the Spirit. He or she does not flaunt moral duty but lives a life of "head, heart, and hands" for the empowerment, healing, and growth of others. This empowerment may not be easily measurable, and it is not synonymous with self-sacrifice. Human beings who are fully alive give of themselves, but they do not give themselves away. They give of themselves by being in relationship, not by remaining isolated so that when a relationship is needed it feels as if something was lost in the transaction.

This way of being friends in the world means that pastors are present to God, their people, and themselves. Using this kind of embodied language helps us see ourselves as whole human beings and not just minds. How pastors understand themselves as human beings, as well as ordained ministers, influences how they practice ministry.

## Pastoral Practice

### Being Friends in the Church

The main problem with a friendship paradigm according to some is that when they need a minister, people, especially in times of crisis, do not want a friend, they want a pastor. Inherent in this comment is an unstated view of what friends are and what pastors are. I prefer to use the word "who" instead of "what" when asking about friends and pastors because when we use "what," we really want to know *what* that person *does*. When we use "who," we really are asking *who* that person *is*. By reframing the question as "who is . . . ?" we can move away from a task orientation to a relational perspective. We can move away from thinking only about what a pastor will do for us and begin to think about the relationship we have with our pastor, what our expectations are, and who this person is. So who is a friend and who is a pastor?

A friend is someone who is there for you, someone you can talk to, someone you trust. He or she is someone who values you, someone who knows you well and tells you the truth. A friend is also someone you love and respect. This description fits a pastor. But for some, the "pastor, not a friend" perspective still remains. What does this mean? For the pastor it means looking for friends, "seeking a third," outside the congregation. For the people who want a pastor and not a friend, it means that they are looking for a person of power and authority who is stronger, more knowing, or closer to God than they are. They want to remain dependent children rather than grow into faithful adults, human beings who are fully alive.

A friend, though, is a person who is vulnerable, and a vulnerable pastor may be seen as a weak pastor. But, "vulnerable" is also a description of God. Jesus Christ has shown us a new way of understanding God. God is vulnerable in love. Theologian William Placher persuasively argues for this understanding of God, an understanding that replaces old notions of absolute power with new notions of vulnerable love.[1] Those who persist in not wanting pastors as friends do so in part because they do not think that a pastor as friend can "do the job." But then there were those folks who did not want women as pastors because they supposedly could not do the job either. This paradigm shift from task to relationship, from power to love is based in the self-revelation of God. We are to be no longer servants but friends, no longer to be defined by power but by love. Jesus tells us this.

We inevitably get into problems in our culture when we talk about love. We are brought up in the church to see love either as *agape* or *eros*. *Agape* is the self-sacrificing love that Jesus displayed by dying on the cross to save us from our sins. *Eros* is used as a synonym for "sexual," but it also means "to possess the beautiful." Our love is either self-sacrificing or sexual, and it does not take a rocket scientist to figure where our culture places women and where it places men. As we saw in earlier chapters, we tend to view love as a relationship between two people, be they husband and wife, parent and child, lovers, or friends. But love to be love must "seek a third." So, thinking with this idea of seeking a third, we find another way. We find *philia*.

When we see love as *philia*, that is, as friendship, we "seek a third." This is not a new idea although it might be a novel one for some.[2] One example is that two persons can become better friends when they include Jesus Christ as "the third" in that relationship. One way that this works is that they each see Christ in each other. This enables them to treat each other with more love and respect, to take care in what they say and do, and to be more intentional in helping the other be the very best person he or she can be.

Another example of seeking a third is to put the face of Christ on someone you are meeting for the first time, on that person who said something that hurt your feelings last week, or on that person who you absolutely cannot stand. Putting the face of Christ on someone who is not your friend enables you to treat that person as a friend, even though the relationship may not be reciprocated. Both of these examples of friendship include God because love, to be love, includes God, and God empowers a friend to be a friend to another. So friendship is a larger concept than someone you hang out at the mall with, or someone you eat lunch with, or someone you telephone frequently or share your confidences with. Friendship as it is used here means seeking a third in love as Father / Mother, Son, and Spirit of the Trinity seek each other and us.

### "Either / Or" Thinking

We began with "either / or" or dichotomous thinking, that something is either this or that. Where does this kind of thinking come from? Dichotomous thinking is deeply ingrained in western culture. The ancient Greek philosopher Plato is famous for what has been called the mind-body split. Plato regarded the mind as real and eternal. The body (and the material world with it) was only an ephemeral appearance and therefore of no value. Others throughout our history recast this division of reality into hierarchies of value. Some elevated the spirit, calling it good, and denigrated the body, calling it evil. Still others privileged male over female, white over black, rich over poor. So part of our cultural baggage is a basic tendency to divide reality into twos in order to understand ourselves. Jesus is calling us to think in threes in order to more adequately understand and experience God, our neighbors, and ourselves.

Today one reason this kind of thinking continues is power. Power shows its shape when we explore how relationships are configured. This is why a paradigm shift from power to love is so important.

Some would say necessary. Love equalizes, promotes freedom and autonomy, and shares decision making. Power, when it is configured as control, does quite the opposite.

Control is a very significant part of the dichotomous thinking that we are addressing. Control is about how one uses power to maintain position and authority. The one who has the power can both make and enforce the rules. A classic power distinction is "power over" and "power within."[3] "Power over" is the power of the servant or the servant leader that is used over or against others. "Power within" is claiming one's identity as made in the image of the triune God. It enables a person to befriend another.

## Friends in Ministry

The new theology of ordained ministry, and the paradigm it generates, offers a real alternative to the paradigms of servanthood and servant leadership by proposing a way that can actually be lived out in the church and its ministries today. How these relationships are constructed and practiced is paramount because how pastors relate to their congregations affects the entire life of the church. Members of our congregations are telling us that they want ordained ministers to relate to them in a different way when they remind us (with smiles on their faces) that we ordained ministers "only work on Sundays." For many of our parishioners, this is the only time they see us! This is the only time they relate to us until a crisis hits.

We now have a new theology of ordained ministry that offers a way to shape our identity as pastors and our practice of ministry that is relational. This is imperative because a theology of ordained ministry, whether explicit or implicit, affects how decisions are made, how people get along, how worship happens, who does ministry and why, the place of education in the church, stewardship, youth, mission, and so on. Where we see this most clearly in the daily life of a congregation is in terms of what we will call "attitudes and styles of ministry." Following are some snapshot illustrations of real pastoral situations that show how the approach of both the servant and servant leadership paradigms compare with the friendship paradigm. The illustrations are of working with groups, pastoral care, worship, and Christian education.

## Snapshot Comparisons

### *Working with Groups*

The new friendship paradigm for ordained ministry contributes to congregational life in the three ways mentioned above: it is relational, communal, and participatory. Its focus is on people and not on tasks. When it comes to working with groups, the pastor who follows the friendship paradigm is relational, that is, he or she "clues people in" about what is going on. Information is power. People who want to maintain control do not share information freely. Communication, then, in the friendship paradigm is lively and widespread, encouraging diverse perspectives and approaches. Therefore, an issue is not settled beforehand. Everyone feels included in the process because the pastor is communal. Members of different groups in the church are included in the process. Shared decision making means the pastor is participatory. However, the servant / servant leader paradigms display a different pattern.

One pastor I know fits the friendship paradigm very well. This pastor put together the yearly stewardship campaign by doing two important things. First, every discussion of finances began with prayer. The prayer was not for more money but for the congregation to be the church that Jesus Christ wanted them to be. Second, there was constant, open sharing with the congregation about the financial state of the congregation. The sharing began with a structure that encouraged all who wished to be included.

A committee (that was not chaired by the pastor) was formed to take a serious look at the financial health of the congregation and report back to the church.

One of the questions they were to investigate was, How has the church supported itself in the past? The group found some very helpful information. First, they discovered that there was one person, now deceased, who was counted on to bail them out in a crisis. Second, membership was down (as in so many churches), so members would need to give more to have the ministry that God was calling them to. While this group was doing its work, detailed information about their findings was presented to the congregation in the monthly church newsletter as well as Sunday morning updates from members of the finance committee. And, there were regularly scheduled (and advertised) open meetings with the leaders of the church to talk things over.

The pastoral emphasis during this entire process of several months was an upbeat "What kind of church is Jesus Christ calling us to be?" It was not "What can we afford?" or "What will we have to do without?" Alongside the finance committee's work, there was also a group of volunteers praying especially for that committee and the future direction God wanted for the church. God and the church's members controlled the process. The pastor gave guidance and kept reminding them to seek Christ's vision for the congregation.

Where the friendship paradigm calls for relating, the servant / servant leader paradigm focuses on maintaining control. As a consequence, a servant / servant leader does not divulge information easily. You might have to track down a servant / servant leader to find out what you want to know. In terms of diversity, the servant / servant leader is monocultural. There is only one persective, one way to get things done. The servant / servant leader is hierarchical and limits participation in decision making to the inner circle. But the servant / servant leader is most often a Lone Ranger, one who makes all the real decisions from the top down. As a church member, you may be left wondering why you even bother trying to participatc in the first place.

Another pastor I know fits the servant / servant leadership paradigm very well. The wide difference between this pastor and the one discussed above will be obvious. The servant / servant leader pastor also put together the annual stewardship campaign, but this pastor did not communicate its design or goals in any detailed way to the congregation. Rarely was any information given to the people. There was nothing in the newsletter of any worth, no public forums, no Sunday updates. It was not clear who was doing what or why. In fact, church members who had successfully spearheaded efforts in the past were systematically excluded from participating. Instead, a few church members who shared the pastor's views ran the campaign. There was no concern for what God wanted the church to be; the pastor had already figured that out alone. There were no prayers for the committee of cronies or the direction in which God was leading the church. Church members found out about the campaign when they got their annual stewardship letter and pledge card in the mail.

On the surface, the friendship paradigm seems less efficient and much more time consuming because it strives to include as many people as possible. But what you may lose in efficiency, you gain in trust and the empowerment of people. The friendship paradigm is noteworthy in that all participate at the level they choose. The servant / servant leader paradigm is less efficient in the long run, for the servant / servant leader trusts neither the people nor the process when it comes to decision making. The servant / servant leader bears the burden alone. Therefore, working with a servant / servant leader often means that you have no idea what was the basis for any decision; let alone whether or not it was the best one.

Which style of ministry benefits congregational life, and which one hinders it, the friendship or the servant / servant leader paradigm? The first pastor's stewardship campaign was a success because it enabled the church to identify the direction that God was calling them toward, which motivated the church members to take a little more seriously their privilege to be partners with God in ministry. The second pastor's campaign was not nearly as successful. No direction for ministry was identified, and people who were not allowed to participate were blamed for the failure.

## Caring for People

Pastoral care means both dealing with people at times of crisis and getting to know people generally, and, as such, pastoral care responsibilities weigh heavily on most pastors. Here again the difference between the friendship paradigm and the servant / servant leader paradigm is obvious because the pattern of relating remains fairly consistent. The pastor who follows the friendship paradigm takes the time to listen, to hear what is going on with the person, paying particular attention to body language to determine if what is being said is really what is going on. This kind of pastor meets that person where she or he is. In other words, the pastor who adopts this paradigm takes the person's context seriously. When the person in need expresses concerns or feelings, they are not judged but heard. The pastor discusses them with the person to determine which ones really fit the situation. Along with this reality check, the pastor can also talk over with the person the kinds of things he or she does to help when such concerns or feelings develop. In this way the pastor aids the person in remembering or discovering the tools they have within themselves to help themselves. This pastor values the whole person. The pastor, knowing his or her own limits, refers to a professional counselor when necessary.

I know a pastor who treats people this way consistently. This pastor is a splendid example of the friendship paradigm. There is an energy, a vitality, and deep love and respect for people in this pastor that can be both seen and felt. People enjoy being around this kind of person not only because of the energy but also because this pastor is willing to be vulnerable, to be human.

There is, of course, the other kind of pastor paradigm. The pastor who follows the servant / servant leader paradigm is more interested in getting something accomplished than in getting to know people. One way of describing this style is the "diagnose it and get over it" school of pastoral care. This kind of pastor does not take the time to listen, does not take feelings seriously, and leaves you to figure out and deal with your concerns and feelings and problems. The whole person is not valued, only what the person can do for the pastor or for the church. Feelings are ignored since they only get in the way of accomplishing the task. Unlike the pastor who follows the friendship paradigm, the servant / servant leader paradigm allows pastors to ignore persons' intentions. Only their actions matter. In other words, the emphasis is on what they did, not why they did it. Such a pastor is inflexible in dealing with people since they are pawns for the pastor's vision and agenda.

This pastor does not even greet you when you arrive, appearing strangely out of touch with people and unconcerned about you. The pastor's face masks rather than reveals who he or she is. There is no gravitational pull to this person that leads people to want to be in his or her presence. The pastor is all business and curt.

### Worship

Worship is another area where the contrast between pastors who follow the friendship paradigm and the servant / servant leader paradigm is clear. Historically, Protestant worship has been very auditory and word oriented. This is evident in the importance put on reading Scripture out loud, preaching, and hymn singing. While there certainly is nothing wrong with this, since we are dealing with the word of God, such a structure can be used to exclude or diminish the other elements of worship and therefore the people who benefit from them. When it comes to the people who attend any given worship service and how they process an experience, 70 percent of them are visual, 20 percent are auditory, and 10 percent are kinesthetic. A worship service needs to speak to each of the three groups to be truly meaningful.

The pastor who is a friend includes something in worship that will address each of the ways people process experience. In many Protestant churches there is little to appeal to the visual sense in people. Communicating through color and design as well as through sacred objects can make a real difference. The vestments or stole of the preacher as well as colorful and simply designed banners can be helpful. On communion Sundays, using a loaf of bread that is large enough to be seen and pouring wine or grape juice from a pitcher into the cup are meaningful visual and auditory cues that remind the participant that communion really is a meal. Another visual aid is the bulletin. Clear notations in the Sunday bulletin guide people through the service and educate them about the meaning of the different parts of worship.

We might assume that since Protestant worship is so auditory it will take care of itself. But the pastor who is a friend knows that the focus is not on what she or he says or on what the choir sings. The focus should be on the hearer, not the speaker. Therefore, pastors who are friends spend time teaching readers to read clearly so that they can be understood when they read out loud. Even the best sound systems will not help if the reader slurs his or her words. And if the acoustics in the sanctuary are less than wonderful, it is all the more important to prepare and take seriously the listener's ability to hear the speaker. The sixteenth-century reformer Martin Luther reminds us that faith comes by hearing the word preached. Hearing means more than listening to sounds; it is a means by which God communicates to us. If we cannot hear what is being said, we surely will not be able to receive God's message.

The kinesthetic side of worship is the least appreciated by Protestant pastors. A quick run-through of a Sunday worship service reveals that most people either sit or stand, or, in some denominations, kneel occasionally. Otherwise, there is very little movement in the sanctuary. Walking to your seat before the service does not count! Pastors who are friends appreciate that people have bodies and need to move them in worship. Some pastors experiment with liturgical dance, but dance is still suspect as a means of worship for some. Other pastors involve their people physically by designing worship services where the people have to get up out of their pews and come forward for communion, renewal of baptismal vows, a healing touch, or blessing. This kind of liturgical activity helps to lessen the almost inevitable "spectator" or "pew potato" aspect of Sunday morning worship. These suggestions show how pastors who adopt the friendship paradigm take their parishioners seriously and make the effort to design worship in a way that takes into account the visual, auditory, and kinesthetic ways people get involved in experience.

Pastors who are friends also do not exclude youth or children from the congregation's worship. Styles of music are often a bone of contention in churches. What the youth like rarely sounds good on an organ. But to reach all the people of God, pastors need to encourage everyone to respond to the good news. One form this encouragement takes is the use of different music styles. The church simply cannot afford to maintain a style at the expense of the good news. Like youth, children need also to be reached. The Sunday morning worship service should not be so exclusively adult that there is nothing in it for kids to relate to. The obvious children's sermon is one example of what can be and has been done, but there needs to be more. Including children as participants presents today's pastor a real challenge and a real opportunity. Worship cannot remain an adult event, which is what servant / servant leaders want to maintain because of their emphasis on the rational, on individualism, and their need to control. We all know what can happen with children in the sanctuary!

It is difficult for many of us to imagine worship different from what we are used to. Pastors experience the fallout from congregations when they change something in worship for just this reason. Some churches deal with the need for different styles of worship today by having two worship services, the so-called traditional and the so-called contemporary. This is not what I am referring to. I am not suggesting that the pastor who decides to minister according to the friendship paradigm start another worship service. In many cases this is not possible under the best of circumstances. However,

I know a pastor who routinely includes people by the way sacraments are celebrated, the hymns that are chosen, and the general tone of the service.

Some pastors bury their faces in worship books during communion. Others never look up from their sermon manuscripts. In both instances, there is no eye contact between the pastor and the people. Or there are those pastors who read through the service so fast that you cannot understand it. Some other pastors make up the service as they go along so that you cannot follow it. Unlike them is a pastor I know who is the minister to a small congregation. This pastor takes the time to clearly enunciate the words of institution from memory while holding up the communion elements for all to see. Then, the pastor smiles during the distribution of the communion elements as the congregation comes forward to receive! Included in the Sunday service hymn choices are congregational favorites, and once a month the congregation learns a new hymn out of the new hymnal. In addition there is a lay reader each Sunday, and children and youth find themselves addressed in the sermon, often with an example about school or one of the concerns that they have today. The general tone of the service begins before the service, when the pastor greets members of the congregation with a smile, looking straight into each face. It is not too difficult to image the antithesis of this pastor. Even in denominations that have a suggested order of worship, particular liturgies for baptism and communion, the pastor works with or against God in the tone he or she sets.

## Christian Education and Youth Ministry

Much of what had been said so far with regard to working with groups, caring for people, and inclusiveness in worship also pertains to Christian education and youth ministry. One of the differences among the paradigms that is worth pointing out, however, is how program driven the church has become. I am not against this except when the people are lost and the program is the priority.

Whether it is with adults, children, or youth, pastors would be well advised not just to teach but to find opportunities to "hang out" with whatever group they are teaching. This relationship orientation that comes with the friendship paradigm is critical in ministry, because getting to know your people, whatever their age group, is vital and enjoyable! So many pastors dismiss youth and children because they do not serve on committees, they do not vote on issues of importance to the congregation, and they do not pay the bills. But as all Christian educators know, handing over the faith to youth and kids so that they will grow into mature Christian adults is one of the main reasons why the church exists in the first place.

I know a pastor who hangs out really well. This pastor goes where the people are and does not wait for them to come to the office. Hanging out means visitation. It means going to homes, shopping malls, or the street—to wherever adults, youth, and kids congregate. And it is letting them know that you are there, that you are available. There is no agenda other than that, no program, no expectations, no demands. You are there. You can be trusted. You are a friend.

## Suggesting Some Ideas for an Ecclesiology

It is not the purpose of this section to offer a complete discussion about the nature and purpose of the church. In keeping with my methodology of collaborative theology, my intention here is to suggest some ideas about the church that are in keeping with the new theology of ordained ministry and its corollary friendship paradigm. When rethinking ordained ministry as servanthood or servant leadership, it is also vital that theological discussions about the church take place on the local level as well as on the academic or judicatory planes. Current discussions about the nature and purpose of the church often begin with biblical descriptions of the church as the Body of Christ, or they pay particular attention to the four marks of the church stipulated in the Nicene Creed. This creed tells us that the church is "one, holy, catholic, and apostolic."[4] I want to focus on the church as the Body of Christ that reveals the Trinity and shares its ways of relating as "a community of equals united in mutual love."

Any ecclesiology that takes seriously this new theology of ordained ministry and adopts its paradigm must first be rooted in the Trinity. As we have seen, the Trinity is the basis for understanding who God is, ourselves as made in the image of God, ordained ministry, and now the church. From the trinitarian pattern we have used, we can suggest a new view of the church that is also made in the image of the Triune God.

We often think of the church in terms of polity, or how it is governed. So some will configure the triadic structure of the church in terms of the offices of bishop, presbyter (elder), and deacon. I am more interested in configuring the church in the structure and ways of relating that I have been calling "head, heart, and hands." Rather than focus on the inevitable hierarchy that comes with governing, body imagery helps to remind us that since the church is the Body of Christ on earth, the church also needs to intentionally embody its theology in word, sacrament, and ministry. Paul writes a lengthy passage in chapter 12 of his First Letter to the Corinthians about how the church needs to see itself as a body, specifically the Body of Christ, and not as a loose assemblage of different gifts, services, and activities. He deftly uses body imagery to show how the members of the church are connected and interdependent. One selection from this passage will demonstrate this:

> For just as the body is one and has many members, and all the members of the body, though many, are one body, so it is with Christ. For in the one Spirit we were all baptized into one body—Jews or Greeks, slaves or free—and we were all made to drink of the one Spirit. (1 Cor. 12:12-13)

Since the church is in so many ways vast and diffuse, the human tendency is to locate the church in one denomination, one congregation, or one pastor. Each in turn is sometimes spoken of as "representing" the church. In particular, pastors are often described as having a "representative" ministry. To some they are supposed to represent the whole church in public functions, for example. What this means is that they themselves embody the whole church. I disagree. Pastors neither speak for the whole church nor do they represent it. They can say what, in their understanding, the church believes regarding a specific doctrine or teaching, or what stand it takes on a particular issue. In other words, pastors can interpret the church to others. However, it is all baptized Christians who represent the church to the world, for together they are the Body of Christ. The pastor is a member of that body. Therefore, the public ministry of Jesus Christ is now the public ministry of the Body of Christ, not just of the servant, or the servant leader, or even the friend.

It is the community together—the church, the Body of Christ—that creates faithful individuals, and not the other way around. This relational bias states that we know ourselves in relationship, not in isolation. This is one reason, along with Paul's understanding of the Body of Christ, that pastors cannot be viewed as isolated servants or servant leaders. They must be friends. Pastors must be connected and interactive with the rest of the Body of Christ. This is crucial for a ministry of word and sacrament, which by definition only can occur where two or more are gathered in Christ's name. I often tell my students that if they want to go home after class and have a communion service in the living room by themselves, it will not be communion.

Because the context is the whole church, the Body of Christ, ordained ministers are not only to preside at the sacraments of baptism and communion, they are also to be formed by them. Baptism is not only an individual becoming part of Christ's Body, the church, but also the church remembering and reaffirming God's presence and grace in their life together. Communion is not only an individual being nourished by the bread of heaven and the cup of salvation, but also the church remembering and reaffirming its unity and interrelatedness. Sometimes when pastors preside at worship, they forget or neglect these deeper meanings. They forget because they are focused on the details of the service, the time it is taking, or perhaps a tiny mistake that happened. But the real focus as the Body of Christ is in celebration with the triune God, the Father / Mother, the risen Christ, and the Holy Spirit—along with the persons present and all who believe, the cloud of witnesses. Without this gathering, worship itself cannot occur. So pastors, like their people, are to enjoy the new life of friendship that these sacraments embody. This new life is a living relationship with the Trinity and the community of faith rather than a life of moral duty as exemplified by the servanthood paradigm or a life of achievement and control as modeled by the servant leader paradigm.

The church, then, as the Body of Christ, embodies the paradigm of head, heart, and hands in its identity and practice. The faith of each member, and the church as a whole, seeks understanding. The seeking happens not only in the study of scripture but also in dialogue with others. Attending to sermons and Bible study classes is vital. This use of the *head* is "reaching up" to God. The prayer of each member and the church as a corporate body, "reaches inward" with the Holy Spirit to get the *heart* of faith pumping, energizing it rather than wearing it out. The "exercise" of prayer also makes the *head* clearer and the *hands* stronger. Attending public worship is of paramount importance. The person of faith and the Body of Christ "reach out" to God and then to the world, with open hands so that the Holy Spirit can pour through them to befriend the world. The pastor's benediction and the people's prayer and blessing response should be a posture that reaches with hands outstretched.

# APPENDIX A

## "NO LONGER SERVANTS, BUT FRIENDS"
## A SERMON BASED ON JOHN 15:12-17

### I. GREETING

Grace and peace to you from our Lord Jesus Christ. It is a great joy to be with you tonight, this night of revival and renewal, and share with you this message. I want to thank your pastor, Allen Gharet, for inviting me. Let us pray. May the words of my mouth and the meditations of all our hearts, be acceptable to you, O God, our rock and our redeemer. Amen.

### II. INTRODUCTION

There is a persistent image in Western civilization that is deeply ingrained in us about how we are to live our lives. The image is that of *master* and *servant* or *slave*. I say *servant* or *slave* because the Greek word used in our New Testament lesson today has been translated both ways. But the meaning of the word really means *slave*. Now, remember that a master has total control over a slave. A master owns a slave. And a slave is really no better than an animal; the slave has no rights, no dignity, no freedom. This master / slave relationship can be found in ancient Israel, Greece, Rome—and it still exists in some places in the world today.

As Americans, we have not been exempt from living as masters and slaves. A little more than 130 years ago, President Abraham Lincoln ended slavery in our country, when with one stroke of the pen he signed the Emancipation Proclamation. But we can still think this way—that some are masters and some are slaves.

I teach at Phillips Theological Seminary. And this image has even infiltrated the school. Some are seen as *masters* and others are seen as *slaves*. Although it is humorous, sometimes we teachers are seen as masters and the students see themselves as slaves. Students see us teachers as commanding them to read books and write papers, which they must then slave over.

## III. THESIS

This way of living as masters and slaves has even infiltrated the church! Some church folk view *pastors* as *slaves*. And some pastors see the *congregation* as the *master*. And, sometimes it's the other way around.

But hear the good news! Jesus Christ is doing a new thing. He is proclaiming a *new relationship*. We are *no longer servants, we are no longer slaves, but friends!* Jesus tells us that we are to love one another as he has loved us. He tells us that we are his friends and that we are to be friends to one another. But, what is a friend? Think for a moment. Think for a moment. Picture in your mind the face of your friend. This person is someone who is there for you—someone you can talk to. He or she is someone who values you, someone you know well and who knows you well, too. She or he is someone you want to spend time with, because your friend is someone you love, someone you respect, someone you trust, someone who tells you the truth.

Did you know that you now have a new friend and that friend is Jesus Christ? Do you know that you are his friend and that he is yours? Did you know that you have a lot of friends? Everybody in this church is your friend. This is what John 15:12-17 is talking about. Jesus Christ and the United Methodist church in Thomas, Oklahoma, are called to love each other—to be friends to each other. But it doesn't end there. We are called to love each other so that God's friendship can be shown to the world.

## IV. APPLICATION

A revival and renewal week like this is a very good time to remember that we are no longer servants but friends. It is a very good time to recall that we are a "chosen race, a royal priesthood, a holy nation" of friends, not masters or slaves (1 Pet. 2:9). As friends, we are equal. We are connected, we are knit together in Jesus Christ. And, as friends, there is more than this! We know what Jesus knows! And how do we know what he knows? How do we know what the Father has told him?

—We know because we have Scripture, the Word of God.

—We know because we have each other, the Body of Christ.

—We know because we have the Holy Spirit, the advocate promised by Jesus, who helps us discern the way, the truth, and the life.

And since Jesus calls us friends, the Holy Spirit helps us to be just that—folks who love one another as Jesus has loved us. And with that love, all of us together are to go out and *befriend the world*.

As Mother Teresa of Calcutta has taught us by her example, every person, no matter his or her station in life, is a friend because God loves everyone.

Jesus Christ is doing a new thing in this church with you and your pastor, Allen! On the one hand, your pastor, Allen, as a friend, won't *lord it over* the congregation. And you, the congregation, also as friends, won't have a *slavish attitude* that only focuses on the daily details of this particular building. On the other hand, pastor Allen won't be self-absorbed in his own worth and work: and you, the congregation, won't be chained to controlling the outcome of everything. Christian life is bigger than this! In this new relationship given by Christ, both Allen and you, pastor and people of God, are free to be friends, to love each other as Christ loves all of us. This means that we are free to work with each other and not against each other, bringing the love of Christ, the love of friends, to those beyond these walls.

Again, as Mother Teresa has taught us, love does not live within church walls. It must be taken into the street and into the towns and given away.

This week, as you move through this time of revival and renewal, gather together as the friends of Jesus Christ, and:

—Let each one of us remember that we are connected to each other and Jesus Christ as friends.

—Let each one of us remember that together in Jesus Christ, we go about ministry, extending love and the glad hand of friendship to the world beyond this sanctuary.

—Let each one of us remember that once we were no people

and now we are God's people, the people who are to proclaim God's wonderful actions to the world. Once we were no people, now we are God's people who have received mercy—the heart of God in Jesus Christ, who now calls us to be friends and not masters or servants, and to share Christ's friendship with the world.

Let us pray: *May the Father, Son, and Holy Spirit be with you, as you and Allen open the doors of this church to befriend the world, sharing God's love with everyone. Amen.*

# APPENDIX B

## GUIDELINES FOR A COMMENTARY ON YOUR DENOMINATION'S ORDINATION SERVICE

**Introduction:** This paper is an exercise in interpretation and understanding. When you understand your denomination's ordination service, what it is saying and doing, you will be able to (1) make an informed choice about whether or not you want to seek ordination, (2) enter more fully into the service during your own ordination, (3) interpret the theology and practice to your church members, and (4) write about ordination for the larger church.

**Method:** For research on the history and context of your ordination service, do not hesitate to set up an appointment with your denominational formation director, area staff, or other members of your denomination for background. For research into the other areas of ordination and worship, consult the work of James F. White, for example, *Introduction to Christian Worship* (revised edition), *A Brief History of Christian Worship, and Documents of Christian Worship: Descriptive and Interpretive Sources.*

The questions listed below should govern your thinking about the ordination service. You may not be able to answer all of them, because some presuppose both attendance at an actual service of ordination and conversation with participants. However, if you remember any details from services previously attended, feel free to add and reflect on them in your commentary. Be sure to note which ordination service it was, where, and when.

**Of special note:** Look at the ordination service not as a group of isolated parts but as interlocking components. Ask yourself how they relate to one another. Each component helps you understand the other components. Pay attention to details.

Your commentary should be 20 to 25 double-spaced pages, with footnotes / endnotes as necessary. If you need an extra page or two, that is fine. Remember to write up your commentary as a *flowing narrative* and not in the outline form of these guidelines.

## Questions

### Background

I. History

1. When was this service of ordination written?
2. Can you identify who wrote it? Give the name and position / title of the author, the committee or commission, and so forth.
3. What was going on in your denomination when this particular service of ordination was written? Concerns? Celebrations?
4. What rationale does your denomination give for ordination?

II. Sources

1. Is there any previous *twentieth-century* service that your service borrows or departs from?
2. Is there anyone in your denominational structure who is an authority on the theology and practice of ordination? If yes, who is it?
3. What biblical passages are highlighted in the text?
4. What, if any, contemporary theological concern serves as a background to the text, for example, inclusive language, ecumenical dialogues, the ordination of women?

### Context

III. Environment / Space

1. Where does the ordination service take place? What does this space look like? Be very specific.
2. When does the service take place? Be specific as to day and time. Is there a customary time during the year?

IV. Liturgical Roles

1. How is the service conducted? Who takes leadership? How many leaders are there and why? What are they doing?

2. Who is in the assembly? Members, friends, the curious?
3. What cultures or racial / ethnic groups are represented in the assembly? How does the service reflect (or not) their presence?
4. How much of the service is "liturgy," that is, "the public work of the people"? How does the assembly—the folks gathered—participate in the service? How are they excluded?
5. How much of the service is comprehensible to the assembly? Can they see and hear and grasp what is happening?

*Texts*

V. Written Texts, Symbols, Ritual Actions and Gestures

1. Written Texts

   a. What do the written texts (scripture, hymns, prayers) have to say about ordination? The church that ordains? The person being ordained?
   b. What is the intent of the ordination sermon? Who preaches, and when does it take place in the service?
   c. What is the intent of the ordination vows or promises, and what do they say about the ordinand? The church? God?
   d. What does the ordination prayer tell you?

2. Symbols

   a. What symbols of ordination are involved? What do they mean? Who gives them? When are they given?
   b. Is ordination a symbol of the church? If so, why? If not, why not?

3. Ritual Actions and Gestures

   a. What actions or gestures are involved? Who does what? And to whom? Is the assembly involved? How? In what way? Be specific and pay attention to details.
   b. What is the significance of "the laying on of hands"? Of "kneeling"? Of "greeting"?
   c. Do the rubrics, the directions / choreography, reflect how the ordination is actually done?

*Theological Interpretation of the Liturgy*

VI. Interpretation

1. What is the theology contained in the ordination service?
   a. What is said about God?
   b. Jesus Christ?
   c. The Holy Spirit?
2. What anthropology is contained in the ordination service?
3. What ecclesiology is contained in the ordination service? Who is the church? Who represents the church?
4. Does the service "say what it means" and "do what it says?"
5. What theology of ordination is present in the texts? In the symbols? In the ritual actions and gestures? In the space?
6. How do these components work together or against each other in the service?
7. Who ordains? What is ordination / ordained ministry?
8. What nuances or outright changes, if any, would you propose in the service and / or in the theology of ordination?

# NOTES

## Chapter 1. Thinking About Ordained Ministry

1. See Douglas John Hall's three-volume systematic theology, *Thinking the Faith: Christian Theology in a North American Context* (Minneapolis: Augsburg Press, 1988); *Confessing the Faith: Christian Theology in a North American Context* (Minneapolis: Fortress Press, 1996); and *Professing the Faith: Christian Theology in a North American Context* (Minneapolis: Fortress Press, 1993).

2. Susan Nelson Dunfee, *Beyond Servanthood: Christianity and the Liberation of Women* (Lanham, Md.: University Press of America, 1989).

3. Jacqueline Grant, "The Sin of Servanthood and the Deliverance of Discipleship," in *A Troubling in My Soul: Womanist Perspectives on Evil & Suffering*, Emilie M. Townes, ed. (Maryknoll, N.Y.: Orbis Press, 1993), 199-218.

4. María Isasi-Díaz, "Un Poquito de Justicia—A Little Bit of Justice," in *Hispanic/Latino Theology: Challenge and Promise*, Ada María Isasi-Díaz and Fernando F. Segovia, eds. (Minneapolis: Fortress Press, 1996), 325-39.

5. William C. Placher, *Narratives of a Vulnerable God: Christ, Theology, and Scripture* (Louisville: Westminster John Knox Press, 1994), 73.

6. John Calvin, *Institutes of the Christian Religion*, 4.1.9. Quoted in Daniel L. Migliore, *Faith Seeking Understanding: An Introduction to Christian Theology* (Grand Rapids, Mich.: Wm. B. Eerdmans Publishing, 1991), 204.

## Chapter 2. Servanthood and Jesus

1. H. Richard Niebuhr, *The Purpose of the Church and Its Ministry* (New York: Harper & Bros., 1956), 64.

2. A major theme in Latin American liberation theology is that God has a "preferential option for the poor."

3. Docetism claims that Jesus was solely divine. It denies that Jesus' human mind and body were real; they were, instead, "appearances." For a good discussion of docetism see Linwood Urban, *A Short History of Christian Thought*, Revised and Expanded Edition (New York: Oxford University Press, 1995), 75-77.

4. Arianism, unlike Docetism, emphasizes the humanity of Jesus and his ability to grow spiritually. Though the highest form of humanity, Jesus, because of his ability to change, is an example for all of us. See Urban, pp. 62-64.

5. For an excellent discussion of this, see Thomas Moore, *Care of the Soul: A Guide for Cultivating Depth and Sacredness in Everyday Life* (New York: HarperPerennial Edition, 1994).

6. Urban, *A Short History of Christian Thought*, 77-78.

7. This insight belongs to Pablo Jiménez. See Justo L. González, *Santa Biblia: The Bible Through Hispanic Eyes* (Nashville: Abingdon Press, 1996), 104.

8. Celia Hahn, *Growing in Authority, Relinquishing Control: A New Approach to* Faithful *Leadership* (Washington, D.C.: The Alban Institute, 1994), 105.

9. The origin of the term *womanist* is attributed to author Alice Walker. Womanist thought distinguishes the qualities and concerns of strong, confident black women of every class and background from those of *feminism*, which can be described as a middle-class white woman's liberation movement. *Mujerista* is the term used for the Latina liberation movement. The term comes from *mujer*, which is Spanish for "woman."

10. For a clear and concise summary of the claims and characteristics of liberation theologies see Elizabeth A. Johnson, *Consider Jesus: Waves of Renewal in Christology* (New York: The Crossroad Publishing Co., 1990, 1996), 84-88.

11. Susan Nelson Dunfee, *Beyond Servanthood: Christianity and the Liberation of Women* (Lanham, Md.: University Press of America, 1989), 144.

12. Ibid.

13. Ibid., 150.

14. Ibid., 157.

15. In *A Troubling in My Soul: Womanist Perspectives on Evil and Suffering*, ed. Emilie M. Townes (Maryknoll, N.Y.: Orbis Books, 1993), 199-218.

16. Grant, "The Sin of Servanthood," 205.

17. Taken from Daniel E. Sutherland, *Americans and Their Servants* (Baton Rouge: Louisiana State University Press, 1981), 10-11. Quoted in Grant, 208.

18. Grant, "The Sin of Servanthood," 207.

19. Ibid., 208.

20. Ibid., 209.

21. Ibid., 210.

22. Ibid., 215.

23. In *Hispanic/Latino Theology: Challenge and Promise*, Ada María Isasi-Díaz and Fernando F. Segovia, eds. (Minneapolis: Fortress Press, 1996), 325-39.

24. Ibid., 325-26.

25. Ibid., 335-36.

## Chapter 3. Servant Leadership of the Church

1. Robert K. Greenleaf, *Servant Leadership: A Journey into the Nature of Legitimate Power and Greatness* (New York: Paulist Press, 1977), 13-14.

2. Robert K. Greenleaf, *The Servant as Leader* (Indianapolis: The Robert K. Greenleaf Center, 1991), 7.

3. I am intentionally using the noninclusive noun "men" here, and I will later only use the pronoun "he" to underscore the pronounced male aspects of servant leadership.

4. This view that Jesus' significance is really an example of a way of life, albeit a superb one, rather than its cause and end, carries through into the works of other writers as we will see later in this chapter. These writers specifically want to apply servant leadership to the ordained or pastoral ministry of the church.

5. Greenleaf, *Servant Leadership*, 28-29.

6. Ibid.

7. Ibid., 327.

8. Ibid.

9. Dr. Anderson is Professor of Theology and Ministry at Fuller Theological Seminary.

10. Ray S. Anderson, *The Soul of Ministry: Forming Leaders for God's People* (Louisville: Westminster John Knox Press, 1997), 198.

11. Ibid.

12. Ibid., 201.

13. Ibid., 200.

14. Ibid.

15. Ibid., 201.

16. Ibid.

17. Ibid.

18. Ibid., 202.

19. Ibid., 203.

20. Ibid., 204.

21. Ibid.

22. Bennett J. Sims, *Servanthood: Leadership for the Third Millennium* (Boston: Cowley Publications, 1997), 6.

23. Ibid., 10-11.

24. Ibid., 11.

25. Ibid., 9.

26. Ibid., 12-13.

27. Ibid., 13.

28. Ibid., 16.

29. Ibid., 17.

30. Ibid., 31. We might recall that the gift of the Spirit is the chief modifier for Anderson. For Greenleaf, the chief modifier is ostensibly servanthood, but it really is control.

31. Ibid., 33.

32. Celia Hahn, *Growing in Authority, Relinquishing Control: A New Approach to Faithful Leadership* (Washington, D.C.: The Alban Institute, 1994), 166.

33. Ibid., 167. Italics mine.

## Chapter 4. A New Theology of Ordained Ministry

1. Eugene H. Peterson, "Lashed to the Mast," *Leadership* (vol. 17, no. 1, Winter, 1996), 58.

2. Ibid., 59.

3. Daniel L. Migliore, *Faith Seeking Understanding: An Introduction to Christian Theology* (Grand Rapids, Mich.: Wm. B. Eerdmans, 1991), 63.

4. *Book of Common Worship of The Presbyterian Church (U.S.A.)*, (Louisville: Westminster John Knox Press, 1993), 42-43.

5. Mary Timothy Prokes, *Mutuality: The Human Image of Trinitarian Love* (Mahwah, N.J.: Paulist Press, 1993).

6. William C. Placher, *Narratives of a Vulnerable God: Christ, Theology, and Scripture* (Louisville: Westminster John Knox Press, 1994), 73.

7. Migliore, *Faith Seeking Understanding*, 63.

8. Prokes, *Mutuality*, 22-25. Prokes borrows this idea from the twelfth-century mystic and theologian Richard of St. Victor.

9. Placher, *Narratives of a Vulnerable God*, 73.

10. Migliore, *Faith Seeking Understanding*, 63.

11. James M. Thomas, Jr., *The 7 Steps to Personal Power* (Ponca City, Okla.: The J. Thomas Company, 1992), 76-77.

12. James F. White, *An Introduction to Christian Worship*, rev. ed. (Nashville: Abingdon Press, 1980), 280.

## Chapter 5. A New Paradigm for Pastoral Identity and Practice

1. William C. Placher, *Narratives of a Vulnerable God: Christ, Theology, and Scripture* (Louisville: Westminster John Knox Press, 1994), 3-26.

2. One approach can be found in a short treatise called "On Spiritual Friendship" composed by Aelred of Rievaulx, a twelfth-century monk and abbot. The treatise is published in *The Cistercian World: Monastic Writings of the Twelfth Century*, Pauline Matarasso, trans., Thomas Wyatt, ed. (New York: Penguin USA, 1993).

3. For an example discussion of power in the ministry, see Martha Ellen Stortz, *Pastorpower* (Nashville: Abingdon Press, 1993).

4. See, for example, Daniel L. Migliore's discussion on the marks of the church in *Faith Seeking Understanding: An Introduction to Christian Theology* (Grand Rapids, Mich.: Wm. B. Eerdmans, 1991), 200-205.